Educational Psychologist

Official Publication of the
Division of Educational Psychology of the
American Psychological Association

Volume 35, Number 1, Winter 2000

EDUCATIONAL PSYCHOLOGIST, 35(1), 1

Writing Development: Introduction to the Special Issue

Steve Graham and Karen R. Harris

Department of Special Education
University of Maryland

Writing has a long and storied history. More than 5,000 years ago, the Sumerians devised a system of writing, called cuneiform, that allowed them to list and record goods by using a wedge-shape reed stylus to make impressions on a moist clay tablet. From this initial record-keeping debut, writing has evolved to become one of humankind's most powerful tools (Swerdlow, 1999). Among its many functions, it has provided a flexible medium for artistic, political, spiritual, and self-expression. For example, ideas expressed in writing have been used as a means for both formulating revolution (see Thomas Paine's pamphlet, *Common Sense*) and maintaining national cohesion (see Chairman Mao's *Little Red Book*). Just as important, writing provides an external memory, making it easier for us to remember, analyze, and share our ideas and thoughts. Writing can even have therapeutic effects, as writing about one's feelings can reduce depression, lower blood pressure, and boost the immune system (Swerdlow, 1999).

Although the scientific study of writing has a much shorter history, totaling no more than 100 years, there has been considerable discussion and research during the last 2 decades about the factors that contribute to writing proficiency and its development (Hayes, 1996). It is generally agreed that competence, and ultimately expertise, in writing is dependent on a broad array of cognitive, motivational, social, and contextual factors. In this special issue of the *Educational Psychologist*, the influence of each of these areas is examined. First, Graham and Harris evaluate the proposition that the development of writing competence depends on high levels of self-regulation (see, e.g., models by Hayes & Flowers, 1980; Zimmerman & Riesemberg, 1997) as well as the mastery of low-level transcription skills (see, e.g., arguments by Berninger, Fuller, & Whitaker, 1996), concluding that the available evidence generally supports this thesis. Second, McCutchen presents a developmental model, based on current empirical findings, that describes how multiple sources of knowledge, stored in long-term memory, are coordinated during writing within the constraints of working memory. The focus of the third article shifts from cognitive to motivational factors, as Bruning and Horn consider the conditions that contribute to the development of writing motivation. Fourth, Fitzgerald and Shanahan construct a preliminary developmental model of writing and reading relations, which details the cognitive features or markers that are critical to obtaining proficiency in both of these areas. Finally, Schultz and Fecho examine how social and contextual variables influence writing and its development.

Because of space limitations, not all aspects of writing development could be addressed in this special issue. Even if more space were available, it is important to realize that current descriptions, models, and theories of writing development are incomplete. As Hayes (1996) noted, "Some parts have begun to take definite shape … Other parts are being actively designed and still others have barely been sketched" (p. 1). Taken together, the articles in this special issue provide substance and structure to some of the more important aspects of writing development. It is our hope that they will serve as a springboard for additional discussion, study, and analysis.

REFERENCES

Berninger, V., Fuller, F., & Whitaker, D. (1996). A process model of writing development: Across the life span. *Educational Psychology Review, 8,* 193–205.

Hayes, J. (1996). A new framework for understanding cognition and affect in writing. In C. M. Levy & S. Ransdell (Eds.), *The science of writing: Theories, methods, individual differences, and applications* (pp. 1–27). Mahwah, NJ: Lawrence Erlbaum Associates, Inc.

Hayes, J., & Flower, L. (1980). Identifying the organization of writing processes. In L. Gregg & E. Steinberg (Eds.), *Cognitive processes in writing* (pp. 3 –30). Hillsdale, NJ: Lawrence Erlbaum Associates, Inc.

Swerdlow, J. (1999). The power of writing. *National Geographic, 196,* 110–132.

Zimmerman, B., & Riesemberg, R. (1997). Becoming a self-regulated writer: A social cognitive perspective. *Contemporary Educational Psychology, 22,* 73–101.

Requests for reprints should be sent to Steve Graham, Department of Special Education, University of Maryland, College Park, MD 20742. E-mail: sg23@umail.umd.edu

EDUCATIONAL PSYCHOLOGIST, *35*(1), 3–12

The Role of Self-Regulation and Transcription Skills in Writing and Writing Development

Steve Graham and Karen R. Harris

Department of Special Education
University of Maryland

It is proposed that the development of writing competence depends on high levels of self-regulation and the mastery of low-level transcription skills. Predictions consistent with each of these claims are identified and evaluated. Although the available data are incomplete and many key findings require further replication, the accumulated evidence generally supports both of these propositions.

During the last 2 decades, considerable progress has been made in understanding the processes involved in writing. Despite these advances, current models of writing and descriptions of its development are incomplete. Although many parts of the writing puzzle are fairly well developed, other aspects remain sketchy (Hayes, 1996). This article examines the role of two processes, self-regulation and transcription, that are included as essential components in many recent descriptions of writing (Berninger, Fuller, & Whitaker, 1996; Kellogg, 1987; McCutchen, 1995; Scardamalia & Bereiter, 1986; Zimmerman & Riesemberg, 1997). It is proposed that the development of writing competence depends on high levels of self-regulation and the mastery of low-level transcription skills, such as handwriting and spelling.

Presently, there is much more data on the role of self-regulation in writing than there is on the impact of basic transcription skills. This is probably due to the heavy emphasis placed on the cognitive and self-regulatory aspects of composing in the two models of writing (Hayes & Flower, 1980; Scardamalia & Bereiter, 1986) that were most influential during the 1980s and 1990s, as well as a general de-emphasis on instruction in transcription skills, such as handwriting and spelling, during this same period (Graham & Weintraub, 1996). Even with the greater emphasis on the self-regulatory aspects of writing, the available evidence in both of these areas is incomplete. As a result, our analysis of more traditional empirical data is complemented by anecdotal reports from professional writers to provide a broader

evidentiary base for examining the role of self-regulation and transcription skills in writing development.

WRITING AND SELF-REGULATION

High levels of self-regulation are thought to be important to skilled writing because composing is an intentional activity that is quite often self-planned and self-sustained (Zimmerman & Riesemberg, 1997). In addition, skilled writing is commonly viewed as a difficult and demanding task, requiring extensive self-regulation and attentional control to manage the writing environment, the constraints imposed by the writing topic, and the processes involved in composing (Kellogg, 1987; Ransdell & Levy, 1996; Scardamalia & Bereiter, 1986; Zimmerman & Riesemberg, 1997). These assumptions are reflected in the prominent position that self-regulation is assigned in influential models of the writing process. Flower and Hayes (1980), for example, noted that "a great part of the skill in writing is the ability to monitor and direct one's own composing process" (p. 39). They contended that skilled writing is a goal-directed activity and that writing processes such as planning, sentence generation, and revising must be orchestrated so that the writer can switch attention between these functions and a host of mechanical, substantive, and environmental concerns. According to their model, this is accomplished by a control structure, the *monitor*, which activates and coordinates the interplay among the various elements involved in writing. Somewhat similarly, Scardamalia and Bereiter (1986) employed the construct of *executive control* to account for the self-regulation and volitional processes that occur during writing.

Self-regulation is thought to enhance writing performance in two ways. First, self-regulatory mechanisms, such as plan-

Requests for reprints should be sent to Steve Graham, Department of Special Education, University of Maryland, College Park, MD 20742. E-mail: sg23@umail.umd.edu

ning, monitoring, evaluating, and revising, provide building blocks or subroutines that can be assembled along with other subroutines, such as procedures for producing text, to form a program for effectively accomplishing the writing task (Scardamalia & Bereiter, 1985). Second, the use of these mechanisms may act as change-inducing agents, leading to strategic adjustments in writing behavior (Scardamalia & Bereiter, 1985; Zimmerman & Riesemberg, 1997). When self-regulatory mechanisms, such as planning and evaluating, are incorporated into writing, for example, they generate information that may influence not only their subsequent use, but other cognitive or affective processes as well. To illustrate, the successful use of a planning strategy should increase the likelihood that it will be used in the future. Moreover, continued success in using the strategy is thought to enhance self-efficacy for writing. It is hypothesized, in turn, that a heightened sense of efficacy influences intrinsic motivation, willingness to seek a strategic solution, and eventual literary attainment (Alexander, Graham, & Harris, 1998; Zimmerman & Riesemberg, 1997).

Despite its assumed importance, many of the details and implications of self-regulation are not adequately specified in current models of writing, including description of key processes, the source of motivation to self-regulate, and the factors that nurture or inhibit the development of self-regulated writing (Graham & Harris, 1997b). A notable exception is a model developed by Zimmerman and Riesemberg (1997), as it provides the most fully developed account to date. They defined self-regulation of writing as the "self-initiated thoughts, feelings, and actions that writers use to attain various literacy goals" (p. 76). They proposed that three general categories of processes are used to exert control when writing. These included environmental (i.e., regulation of the physical or social context of writing), behavioral (i.e., regulation of the overt motoric aspects of writing), and personal processes (i.e., regulation of cognitive beliefs and affective states associated with writing). These processes interact reciprocally via an enactive feedback loop, involving a cyclic process in which writers monitor the success of the strategies employed and continue, modify, or abandon what they are doing based on the resulting feedback. The use of these processes is closely linked to one's perceived capabilities (i.e., self-efficacy) to plan and implement the actions necessary to complete successfully the writing task. Furthermore, the importance and use of each form of self-regulation is assumed to vary according to environmental conditions, personal effort, and writing outcomes.

Theorists have identified a variety of self-regulation strategies that writers use to control environmental, behavioral, and personal processes (Graham & Harris, 1994b; Zimmerman & Riesemberg, 1997). These include goal setting and planning (e.g., establishing rhetorical goals and tactics to achieve them), seeking information (e.g., gathering information pertinent to the writing topic), record keeping (e.g., making notes), organizing (e.g., ordering notes), trans-forming (e.g., visualizing a character to facilitate written description), self-monitoring (e.g., checking to see if writing goals are met), reviewing records (e.g., reviewing notes or the text produced so far), self-evaluating (e.g., assessing the quality of text or proposed plans), revising (e.g., modifying text or plans for writing), self-verbalizing (e.g., saying dialogue aloud while writing or personal articulations about what needs to be done), rehearsing (e.g., trying out a scene before writing it), environmental structuring (e.g., finding a quiet place to write), time planning (e.g., estimating and budgeting time for writing), self-consequating (e.g., eating ice cream as a reward for completing a writing task), seeking social assistance (e.g., asking another person to edit the paper), and self-selecting models (e.g., emulating the tactics or style of writing of a more gifted author).

If the use of such self-regulation strategies is an important element in the development of skilled writing, it is reasonable to expect that (a) skilled writers are more self-regulated than less skilled writers, (b) developing writers become increasingly self-regulated with age and schooling, (c) individual differences in self-regulation predict individual differences in writing, and (d) teaching such strategies improves the writing performance of developing and struggling writers. We examine each of these predictions next.

Prediction 1: Skilled Writers Are More Self-Regulated Than Less Skilled Writers

Skilled writers. For the most part, high levels of self-regulation are evident in professional writers' descriptions of how they compose (see, e.g., Burnham, 1994; Lamb, 1997; Plimpton, 1989; Zimmerman & Riesemberg, 1997). In interviews published in the *Paris Review* (Plimpton, 1989), for example, self-initiated strategies for controlling environmental, behavioral, and personal processes were quite common among prominent 20th-century authors. Examples of strategies used to control the physical or social context of writing ranged from Ernest Hemingway's daily routine of composing first thing in the morning because it was quiet and cool to Jack Kerouac's ritual of lighting a candle, writing by its light, and blowing it out once he was done. Behavioral strategies included the generation of voluminous notes and character descriptions by Scott Fitzgerald as well as a general program of multiple revisions by Truman Capote, starting with the revision of his initial handwritten draft, followed by a second revision after typing the composition on yellow paper, and a third revision once it had set for a week or more. Strategies for regulating cognitive beliefs and affective states varied from Thornton Wilder taking a long walk as a motivation to start writing each day to Georges Simenon checking in with a doctor to assure himself that he was up to the demanding task of starting a new book.

Such anecdotal reports by professional writers are supported by more scientific observations of adults who are skilled writers. This can be illustrated by considering the self-regulatory skill of planning. In a study of adult writers who were asked to think aloud while composing, Hayes and Flower (1980) found that almost 80% of content statements produced early in the process of composing focused on planning. Gould (1980) reported that business executives spent about two thirds of their composition time planning. Kellogg (1987) found that college students spent about one fourth of their writing time planning. Although these figures vary considerably and are limited to a single process, they show that self-regulation accounts for a significant amount of the activity in skilled writing. The role of self-regulation in skilled writing is even more prominent when other self-regulatory strategies are included in this tally. For instance, in the study by Kellogg, another 20% of writing time was spent reviewing written ideas, and Hayes and Flower reported that 10% to 15% of content statements involved the process of revision.

It is important to note that some professional writers provide descriptions of the composing process that are at odds with the aforementioned anecdotes and findings. Harriet Beecher Stowe, for instance, had so little idea what was going to happen next when writing *Uncle Tom's Cabin* that she thought that the book was written through her by another hand (Burnham, 1994). Similarly, the novelist Hervey Allen, author of *Anthony Adverse,* believed that he received help from his ancestors and an angel-like creature that danced along his pen while he wrote (Plimpton, 1989). Unlike Stowe and Allen, who relied on a metaphysical recorder to explain how they wrote, other professional writers have claimed that writing occurs through the unconscious mind (see Safire & Safire, 1992, for examples) or have described an approach to writing where planning, revising, and other self-regulatory strategies are not prominent or are notably absent (see Kazin, 1967, for examples). Harold Pinter, the playwright, for instance, noted that he often wrote in a high state of excitement and frustration, with a dim view of a possible overall idea, following what he saw on the paper, one sentence after another (Plimpton, 1989). As Ransdell and Levy (1996) noted, there are times when writing is "fluent, fluid, and seemingly effortless" (p. 93), requiring little in the way of self-regulatory activity.

It is difficult to evaluate scientifically the assertion that a metaphysical recorder guides the writing process or that writing occurs through the unconscious mind. Such assertions, however, have been challenged by other authors, who have either made light of them or offered alternative explanations. For example, in response to Hervey Allen's claim of metaphysical help, James Thurber sarcastically commented that the novelist had all the luck (most of these descriptions are limited to novelists or poets), as humorists such as himself never got any help from their ancestors (Plimpton, 1989). We suspect that some professional writers are able to minimize self-regulatory processes during writing, because these processes have become so routine that they require little con-scious attention. To illustrate, Lillian Hellman, the playwright, indicated that she was able to write without a clear conception of what would happen because she had become so practiced and skilled that the use of self-regulatory strategies, such as advanced planning, were no longer needed (Kazin, 1967).

Developing writers. Developing writers typically show little high-level, goal-directed behavior when composing (McCutchen, 1988; Scardamalia & Bereiter, 1986). They commonly approach writing by converting the assignment into a task of writing as remembering or writing by pattern (McCutchen, 1995). Any information that is somewhat appropriate is retrieved from memory and written down, with each preceding sentence or phrase acting as a stimulus for the next idea. Little attention is directed to rhetorical goals, the constraints imposed by the assignment, the needs of the reader, or the organization of the text. The role of self-regulation strategies, such as planning and revising, are minimized, as this retrieve-and-write process typically functions like an automated and encapsulated program, operating largely without metacognitive control (McCutchen, 1988). This is not to say that this knowledge-telling approach to writing is thoughtless; rather it is primarily forward moving, with little of the recursive interplay among composing processes commonly observed among more skilled writers (Hayes & Flower, 1980).

Although there are few actual comparisons between the self-regulatory processes employed by developing and skilled writers, an investigation by Bereiter and Scardamalia (1987) revealed markedly different levels and patterns between these groups, at least in the area of planning. They found that undergraduate students (i.e., skilled writers) planned their entire composition during a scheduled preplanning period, generating multiple and abbreviated lists of ideas that were connected by lines or arrows. Conceptual planning notes, evaluative statements, and structural markers were also quite common. In contrast, the planning notes developed in advance by children in Grades 4, 6, and 8 showed that younger students simply generated complete sentences that were edited into a final draft when writing, whereas older students listed content ideas that were later worked into their compositions.

As they wrote, the participants in the Bereiter and Scardamalia (1987) study were asked to think aloud. Analysis of the resulting protocols revealed that one third of the planning statements made by the undergraduate students focused on conceptual issues and their content statements were typically concerned with goals, structuring their writing, and overcoming difficulties. Developing writers rarely made such comments. Not surprising, self-regulatory differences between skilled and developing writers are not limited just to planning, as the revising behavior of these two groups differ as well. For instance, skilled writers revise more for meaning and make more sentence- and theme-related changes than their developing counterparts (Fitzgerald, 1987).

Cameron, Hunt, and Linton (1996) raised a challenge to the predicted differences between skilled and developing writers, suggesting that young writers differ little from skilled writers in their text-production capabilities. They indicated that qualitative and anecdotal evidence collected in classrooms that support students' self-regulatory abilities, namely process writing and whole-language classrooms, provide evidence that even young children show high levels of self-regulation and problem solving when composing under favorable conditions. Although we agree that classroom or environmental supports can boost self-regulatory competence, there is little reason to believe that children's self-regulatory skills, even those in process or whole-language classrooms, are a match for those of skilled writers (see Smagorinsky, 1987, for a critical review of ethnograhic and anecdotal evidence concerning process writing; and Graham & Harris, 1994a, 1997c, for reviews of research on whole-language and process writing).

Struggling writers. Consistent with the evidence reviewed so far—that skilled writers are more self-regulated than developing writers—better writers are more self-regulated than their poorer writing peers, at least if data on planning and revising are representative of general levels of self-regulation in writing. Good writers spend more time planning and focus more of their attention on text-level concerns than struggling writers (Humes, 1983), better writers make more revisions than their less competent counterparts (Fitzgerald, 1987), and good writers are more knowledgeable than poor writers about the self-regulatory processes involved in composing (Englert, Raphael, Fear, & Anderson, 1988).

These findings are further supported by several studies conducted by Graham and his colleagues (Graham, 1997; De La Paz, Swanson, & Graham, 1998) that show that the performance of struggling writers may be hobbled by difficulties managing and coordinating the elements underlying the process of revising. In one study (Graham, 1997), fifth- and sixth-grade students who scored 1 *SD* below the mean on a standardized writing test received help directing the revising process by using a routine that insured that the evaluative and tactical decisions involved in revising occurred in a regular way. The routine primarily focused students' attention on sentence-level concerns. In a second study, eighth-grade students with writing scores 1 *SD* below the mean used a similar routine, involving two revising cycles: one focusing on text-level concerns and the other on more local difficulties. In both studies, participants reported that the self-regulatory support provided via the revising routine made the task of revising easier. There was also an increase in the number of revisions that were rated as improving text in both studies, and the overall quality of students' revised text improved as a con-

sequence of using the routine in the second study. Although additional replication is needed with other self-regulatory processes, these investigations provide support that such processes contribute to the difficulties experienced by struggling writers.

Prediction 2: Developing Writers Become Increasingly Self-Regulated With Age and Schooling

Notably scarce in the study of writing are longitudinal investigations tracing the development of self-regulatory processes (Graham & Harris, 1997b). Most current research employs cross-sectional methodology and typically focus on a single self-regulatory strategy or process. Although a great deal remains to be learned about the breadth, depth, and course of self-regulation in writing, the available data generally support the prediction that writing becomes increasingly self-regulated with experience and maturity. For example, in the Bereiter and Scardamalia (1987) study reviewed earlier, the amount of planning notes produced between fourth and sixth grade doubled, whereas conceptual planning increased slightly across the fourth- to eighth-grade range. Similarly, Boscolo (1990) found that most of the planning notes produced by children in Grades 2 and 4 were sentences that were repeated with minor changes when writing, but about 35% of notes in Grades 6 and 8 were either reminders to recall a certain item when writing or superordinate titles that summarized or synthesized information. Although there is considerable individual variation, revising behavior also tends to change with age or experience, with older writers revising more often, revising larger units of text, and making more meaning-based revisions (Fitzgerald, 1987). Finally, students' conceptualization of writing appears to become more self-regulatory with age, at least during early adolescence, as older students were more likely to emphasize the self-regulatory aspects of composing than younger students in two interview studies where participants responded to questions about the process of writing (Graham, MacArthur, & Schwartz, 1993; Wong, Wong, & Blenkinsop, 1989).

Additional research is clearly needed to replicate and expand on these findings. This includes more ambitious, descriptive, and developmental writing studies designed to track the emergence and trajectory of multiple self-regulatory strategies. As writers gain more competence, we anticipate both quantitative and qualitative shifts in their levels of self-regulatory behavior (see Alexander et al., 1998). For instance, self-regulatory strategies that were initially inefficient and inelegant will be upgraded and refined to make them more effective. In addition, the use of some self-regulatory strategies will undoubtedly decline with increased competence no longer being necessary, whereas the frequency and importance of others will increase, as the complexity and difficulty of writing tasks and personal writing goals become more challenging. Without more extensive and longitudinal investigation, however, it will be difficult to develop a comprehensive and integrated theory of writing or to design developmentally appropriate writing practices involving self-regulation.

Prediction 3: Individual Differences in Self-Regulation Predict Individual Differences in Writing

Data from studies examining the relation between writing and self-regulation generally support the prediction that individual differences in self-regulatory behavior predict individual differences in writing performance. These findings must be interpreted cautiously, though, as they are either based on indirect measures (i.e., self-reports) or may be confounded by other intervening variables (see the following discussion).

In a frequently cited study by Englert et al. (1988), students in fourth and fifth grade were asked a series of questions that assessed, among other things, their knowledge of self-regulatory strategies in writing. The task was made more concrete by tying the questions to three vignettes of children who were experiencing difficulty on a particular writing task and asking the participants to give these children advice. Correlations between performance on expository writing tasks and knowledge of 10 different self-regulatory processes ranged from .25 to .70. All but two of the self-regulatory variables, sources of information and revising, were significantly related to writing achievement. Somewhat similar results were found by Bonk, Middleton, Reynolds, and Stead (1990) who reported that a composite measure of knowledge of self-regulatory strategies was significantly related to the overall quality of three papers written by children in Grades 6 through 8 (correlations ranged from .35–.45).

Studies examining the relation between a single self-regulatory strategy and writing performance have focused mostly on revising and planning. Until high school or later, revising behavior is generally unrelated to overall writing performance, probably because younger children do not revise very much and tend to limit their revisions to proofreading and minor word changes (Fitzgerald, 1987). In terms of planning, both quantity and quality of plans are typically related to writing performance. In their review of literature, Hayes and Nash (1996) reported that the correlations between writing quality and amount of planning ranged from .11 to .66 for adults, whereas correlations between quality of writing and quality of plans ranged from .23 to .87 for students in Grade 6 through college. In interpreting these findings, Hayes and Nash cautioned that correlation does not imply causation and that a correlation can be caused by any of a multitude of third factors, or namely a confounding variable. This can create the appearance of a special relation between two variables when none actually exists. In several of the studies they reviewed, for instance, a previously significant correlation between writing quality and planning became nonsignificant

once time-on-task was held constant via the technique of partial correlation.

The issue of time-on-task raised by Hayes and Nash (1996) can also be controlled by holding planning and writing time constant. This was done in a study by Berninger, Whitaker, Feng, Swanson, and Abbott (1996) in which students in Grades 7 through 9 were each provided a constant amount of time to plan and write (10 min for each process). Under these conditions, there was a small but significant correlation (.21) between level of planning and the organization of students' text.

Prediction 4: Teaching Self-Regulatory Strategies Improves Writing

Unlike correlational studies, causation can be implied in experimental studies in which writing performance improves following instruction in self-regulation. Such improvements have been observed for both developing and struggling writers (see reviews by Graham & Harris, 1994b; Harris & Graham, 1996; Zimmerman & Riesemberg, 1997). In some instances, improvement occurred as a result of instruction in the use of a single self-regulatory strategy, such as goal setting (Graham, MacArthur, & Schwartz, 1995; Page-Voth & Graham, 1999) or self-monitoring (e.g., Harris, Graham, Reid, McElroy, & Hamby, 1994). In other cases, improvements were associated with learning to use a heuristic that contained multiple self-regulatory procedures (Sawyer, Graham, & Harris, 1992; Troia, Graham, & Harris, 1999). Although not all of the self-regulation strategies described at the beginning of this article have been the subject of experimental training studies, the array of strategies that have been taught and tested are broad enough to support a general conclusion that increased self-regulation enhances writing performance. Self-regulation strategies that have been used to improve the writing performance of both developing and struggling writers include goal setting and planning, seeking information, organizing, transforming, self-monitoring, self-evaluating, revising, self-verbalizing, and self-selecting models (see Graham & Harris, 1994b; for reviews of individual studies, see Zimmerman & Riesemberg, 1997).

A recent study by De La Paz (1999) illustrated the impact of self-regulation instruction on writing performance. Over a 4-week period, middle-school teachers taught seventh- and eighth-grade students to use a self-regulation heuristic to guide the process of writing essays. The heuristic contained strategies for advanced and online planning, including goal setting, seeking information, and organizing, as well as strategies for monitoring these processes. Instruction in the use of this heuristic had a positive effect on writing performance of good, average, and struggling writers. Their papers became longer, more complete, and qualitatively better.

In summary, the evidence reviewed here supports the claim that the development of writing competence depends on high levels of self-regulation. Although the current research base is incomplete and further replication is needed, the data are generally consistent with our predictions that skilled writers are more self-regulated than less skilled writers, developing writers become increasingly self-regulated with maturity and experience, individual differences in self-regulation predict writing achievement, and teaching self-regulation strategies to developing and struggling writers improves writing performance. This is further supported by recent findings showing that a writer's self-efficacy can be enhanced by the judicious use of a combination of self-regulatory procedures (e.g., Schunk & Swartz, 1993; Zimmerman & Kitsantas, 1999).

TRANSCRIPTION SKILLS

Transcription involves transforming the words that the writer wants to say into written symbols on the printed page (Berninger, Fuller, & Whitaker, 1996). It primarily entails the processes of spelling and handwriting (or typing). Mastery of transcription skills are thought to be important to writing development because the execution of these skills can consume considerable attentional resources, especially if they cannot be carried out fluently and efficiently. For those who have not yet mastered the mechanics of writing, having to consciously attend to the lower level skills of getting language onto paper may tax the writer's processing memory, interfering with higher order skills such as planning and content generation (Graham, 1990). Consistent with this view, McCutchen (1996) proposed that the act of spelling and handwriting are so demanding for young writers that they minimize the use of other writing processes, such as planning and revising, because they exert considerable processing demands as well. Berninger, Mizokawa, and Bragg (1991) further proposed that difficulties mastering transcription skills can lead children to avoid writing and develop a mind-set that they cannot write, leading to arrested writing development.

If transcription skills are an important element in the development of skilled writing, it is reasonable to expect that (a) more skilled writers evidence greater mastery of transcription processes than less skilled writers, (b) the transcription skills of developing writers improve with age and schooling, (c) individual differences in transcription skills predict writing achievement, (d) ignoring or eliminating transcription skills enhances writing performance, and (e) teaching these skills results in improvements in writing. Each of these predictions are examined next.

Prediction 1: Transcription Processes of Skilled Writers Surpass Those of Less Skilled Writers

Handwriting and spelling difficulties have bedeviled a number of professional writers, including such notables as James Joyce and Victor Hugo (Henderickson, 1994). Joyce's handwriting was so bad, for example, that one section of *Ulysses* was mistaken for scrap paper and tossed in the fire. Nevertheless, it is generally assumed that skilled writers enjoy the advantages of having handwriting and spelling largely automated so that they require little conscious attention during composing (Scardamalia & Bereiter, 1986). This is not to say that transcription skills have no influence on the writing of skilled writers. Popular writers, such as Steve Allen and Sidney Shelton, have indicated that they dictate rather than write, as this allows them to compose at a rate closer to their speed of thought (De La Paz & Graham, 1995). As research by Bourdin and Fayol (1993, 1994) demonstrated, however, the transcription processes of skilled writers (i.e., adults) impose little cost on limited writing resources in comparison to the transcription skills of developing writers (i.e., children). They found that adults were equally adept at recalling information and generating sentences when asked to respond orally or in writing, but children's performance was significantly poorer when writing.

For the most part, the handwriting and spelling skills of children who experience writing difficulties are less well developed than the transcription skills of their normally achieving classmates (see, e.g., Deno, Marston, & Mirkin, 1982; Farr, Hughes, Robbins, & Greene, 1990; Graham & Weintraub, 1996). This was illustrated in a longitudinal study by Juel (1988) in which 14 of 21 children in fourth grade who were classified as poor writers scored 1 *SD* below the mean on a standardized test of spelling. Although these data generally support the prediction that the transcription processes of more skilled writers are better developed than those of less skilled writers, additional research is needed to determine more precisely the frequency of transcription difficulties for children who are good, average, and struggling writers.

Prediction 2: The Transcription Skills of Developing Writers Improve With Age and Schooling

There is a considerable body of research showing that spelling improves with age and schooling (see, e.g., Farr et al., 1990; Gentry, 1982; Smith & Ingersoll, 1984). The developmental aspects of spelling are especially evident in young children (Gentry, 1982) as they move through the following stages from preschool to the early elementary years: precommunicative (symbols bear no relation to the sounds in a word), semiphonetic (letters represent some but not all of the sounds in a word), phonetic (complete phonological structure of a word is represented, but often with unconventional orthography), transitional (more conventional orthographic conventions are applied), and correct (grade-level words spelled correctly). Beyond the primary grades, spelling continues to improve, as the percentage of words spelled correctly in children's compositions increases from one grade to the next, at least through Grade 9 (Farr et al., 1990).

Children's fluency with handwriting also improves with schooling and age (for a review of normative data, see Graham & Weintraub, 1996), typically increasing 10 letters or more per minute with each succeeding grade level. Such increases, however, appear to level off by the start of high school, as the speeds of students in Grade 9 approximate those typically obtained by adults (Graham, Berninger, Weintraub, & Schafer, 1998). Although data charting the course of handwriting legibility is less consistent, the writing of young children becomes increasingly legible during the elementary-school years but may plateau or even regress in Grades 4 or later (Graham & Weintraub, 1996), probably because of increasing demands for fluency and personalization of handwriting style. Overall, however, the available data support the prediction that transcription skills improve with age and schooling.

Prediction 3: Individual Differences in Transcription Skills Predict Writing Achievement

Most of the available studies examining the concurrent relation between writing and transcription were summarized recently by Graham, Berninger, Abbott, Abbott, and Whitaker (1997). The most robust finding in their review of 13 studies was that spelling was moderately correlated with writing quality, whereas low to moderate correlations were generally found between spelling and writing output. Handwriting fluency was also moderately correlated with writing performance, but there were too few studies to separate out specific effects. In contrast, handwriting quality was not correlated with measures of composing.

We located three additional studies (not included in the review by Graham et al., 1997) that also yielded results that are generally consistent with the prediction that individual differences in transcription skills predict writing achievement. First, Jones and Christensen (1999) reported that handwriting skills accounted for 50% of the variance in the writing quality of second-grade children when reading scores were held constant. Second, Juel (1988) indicated that spelling performance accounted for 29% of the variance in the writing scores of first-grade children in her longitudinal study when oral production skills were held constant, but this dropped to 10% by fourth grade. One interpretation of this finding is that transcription skills become less important in the intermediate grades. However, the findings from a much larger and comprehensive study by Graham et al. (1997) suggest that this is not the case. Using structural equation modeling, they found that handwriting and spelling skills accounted for a sizable proportion of the variance in the writing skills of children in Grades 1 through 6 and that there was no significant drop in the amount of variance accounted for in the primary versus the intermediate grades. Transcription skills accounted for 25% and 42% of the variance in compositional quality at the primary and intermediate grades, and 66% and 41% of the variance in compositional fluency (amount of text written in a specified period) at these same grade levels, respectively.

Prediction 4: Ignoring or Eliminating Transcription Skills Enhances Writing Performance

One way to experimentally examine the effects of transcription skills on writing is to reduce the demands of specific transcription skills during writing and observe if the planned alterations influence the composing process or resulting product. This was done in a study by Glynn, Britton, Muth, and Dogan (1982). College students were directed not to worry about mechanics (i.e., compliance with spelling and punctuation rules) when generating a first draft of a document. Reducing the demands to attend to transcription skills resulted in an increase in the number of arguments they included in their paper. Unfortunately, the mechanisms responsible for this improvement were unclear, as directions not to worry about mechanics did not influence the number of spelling or punctuation errors made by participants.

A second means for examining the effects of transcription is to simply eliminate the mechanical demands of writing altogether by having writers dictate their composition. In a recent review of studies comparing dictation and writing, De La Paz and Graham (1995) reported that one advantage of removing the mechanical demands of composing is that writers, old and young, usually produce more text. A second advantage that is often obtained with young children just learning to write and older elementary-age children with poorly developed transcription skills (i.e., students with learning disabilities) is that text quality improves as well.

Although these findings support the prediction that eliminating transcription skills enhances writing performance, the impact of transcription on writing may have been underestimated. Participants in many of the studies reviewed by De La Paz and Graham (1995) probably had little or no access to text as it was being dictated and may have viewed dictation as a request to speak extemporaneously. Reece and Cumming (1996) addressed these weaknesses in a series of studies with fifth- and sixth-grade children. Dictated text was made accessible by having it appear on a computer screen as it was generated, and it was emphasized that dictation was not telling a story, but composing it. Text dictated under these conditions were judged to be qualitatively better than those that were handwritten, suggesting that transcription skills can also influence the writing quality of older elementary-grade children as well.

Prediction 5: Teaching Transcription Skills Improves Writing

Although research on the teaching of transcription skills started at the beginning of the 20th century, we were only able to locate three studies that examined the impact of either handwriting or spelling instruction on children's writing. In a study by Berninger et al. (1997), first-grade children at risk for handwriting difficulties were randomly assigned to five handwriting treatment groups or a phonological awareness treatment condition. Performance on a standardized writing test improved for students assigned to the most successful handwriting group. This group wrote each letter from memory after viewing a model of the letter containing directional arrows. A second investigation by Jones and Christensen (1999) found that instruction aimed at improving the letter formation and handwriting fluency skills of first-grade children with poor handwriting enhanced both handwriting and story-writing performance. Finally, Berninger et al. (1998) indicated that spelling instruction that emphasized the learning of common phoneme-spelling associations, practicing new spellings by saying each letter in the word plus the onset and the rime, and using spelling words when writing a short composition resulted in improvements in spelling as well as the number of words produced when writing for second-grade children who were poor spellers. Although these three studies support the prediction that transcription instruction improves writing performance, they provide a relatively meager validation, as they involved only primary-grade students who experienced transcription difficulties, and the investigations did not examine if the observed effects were maintained past the initial instructional period.

In summary, the evidence reviewed in this article not only supports the claim that writing competence depends on high levels of self-regulation, but indicates that writing development is dependent on the mastery of transcription skills as well. The accumulated data are generally consistent with our predictions that more skilled writers demonstrate greater mastery of transcription processes than less skilled writers, the transcription skills of developing writers improve with age and schooling, individual differences in transcription skills predict writing achievement, eliminating transcription skills enhances writing performance, and transcription instruction improves writing. All of these predictions require additional verification, especially the final one, namely, transcription instruction improves writing performance.

The data reviewed in this article are also consistent with the view that writing difficulties, at least in part, are a consequence of problems in acquiring or using self-regulatory processes and transcription skills (Graham, 1999; Graham & Harris, 1997a). The composing of poorer writers is less self-regulated than that of their better writing peers, and their transcription skills are not as well developed. Even more important, the performance of struggling writers can be improved by boosting their level of self-regulation when writing or improving their transcription skills. Thus, both of these processes need to be considered when designing instructional programs for these students.

POSTSCRIPT

In the book, *Steel Beach,* by John Varley (1992), journalists are able to activate an internal recorder and think their story into the external memory of a computer. Although such marvelous writing tools are as yet an invention of the imagination, a more modest revolution is currently underway that may make transcription skills as obsolete as the stone and chisel. This involves the development of speech recognition software that allows writers to speak instead of type or write their compositions. Assuming that the capabilities of this software continue to improve and it becomes commonplace, children of the future may learn to compose without ever, or only rarely, using a pen, pencil, or keyboard. It is doubtful, however, that such a state of affairs will significantly reduce the role of self-regulation in writing. Although future writers will undoubtedly have access to new tools that will assist the process of planning and revising, these and other self-regulatory processes will continue to be a critical cornerstone of skilled writing. This was illustrated on a small scale in a recent study by De La Paz and Graham (1997). They found that students with writing and learning difficulties did their best composing when planning instruction was combined with dictation. Although improved speech recognition software will be a great boon to children such as these, it will not eliminate the need to plan, monitor, evaluate, revise, and so forth.

REFERENCES

Alexander, P., Graham, S., & Harris, K. R. (1998). A perspective on strategy research: Progress and prospects. *Educational Psychology Review, 10,* 129–154.

Bereiter, C., & Scardamalia, M. (1987). *The psychology of written composition.* Hillsdale, NJ: Lawrence Erlbaum Associates, Inc.

Berninger, V., Fuller, F., & Whitaker, D. (1996). A process model of writing development: Across the life span. *Educational Psychology Review, 8,* 193–205.

Berninger, V., Mizokawa, D., & Bragg, R. (1991). Theory-based diagnosis and remediation of writing disabilities. *Journal of School Psychology, 29,* 57–79.

Berninger, V., Vaughn, K., Abbott, R., Abbott, S., Rogan, L., Brooks, A., Reed, E., & Graham, S. (1997). Treatment of handwriting problems in beginning writers: Transfer from handwriting to composition. *Journal of Educational Psychology, 89,* 652–666.

Berninger, V., Vaughn, K., Abbott, R., Brooks, A., Abbott, S., Rogan, L., Reed, E., & Graham, S. (1998). Early intervention for spelling problems: Teaching functional spelling units of varying size with a multiple-connections framework. *Journal of Educational Psychology, 90,* 587–605.

Berninger, V., Whitaker, D., Feng, Y., Swanson, L., & Abbott, R. (1996). Assessment of planning, translating, and revising in junior high writers. *Journal of School Psychology, 34,* 23–32.

Bonk, C., Middleton, J., Reynolds, T., & Stead, L. (1990, April). *The index of writing awareness: One tool for measuring early adolescent metacognition in writing.* Paper presented at the annual meeting of the American Educational Research Association, Washington, DC.

Boscolo, P. (1990). The construction of expository text. *First Language, 10,* 217–230.

Bourdin, B., & Fayol, M. (1993, August). *Comparing speaking span and writing span: A working memory approach.* Paper presented at the meeting of the European Association for Research in Learning and Instruction, Aix-en-Provence, France.

Bourdin, B., & Fayol, M. (1994). Is written language production more difficult than oral language production? A working memory approach. *International Journal of Psychology, 29,* 591–620.

Burnham, S. (1994). *For writers only.* New York: Ballantine.

Cameron, C., Hunt, A., & Linton, M. (1996). Written expression as reconceptualization: Children write in social time. *Educational Psychology Review, 8,* 125–150.

De La Paz, S. (1999). Self-regulated strategy instruction in regular education settings: Improving outcomes for students with and without learning disabilities. *Learning Disabilities Research & Practice, 14,* 92–106.

De La Paz, S., & Graham, S. (1995). Dictation: Applications to writing for students with learning disabilities. In T. Scruggs & M. Mastropieri (Eds.), *Advances in learning and behavioral disabilities* (Vol. 9, pp. 227–247). Greenwich, CT: JAI.

De La Paz, S., & Graham, S. (1997). Effects of dictation and advanced planning instruction on the composing of students with writing and learning problems. *Journal of Educational Psychology, 89,* 203–222.

De La Paz, S., Swanson, P., & Graham, S. (1998). The contribution of executive control to the revising by students with writing and learning difficulties. *Journal of Educational Psychology, 90,* 448–460.

Deno, S., Marston, D., & Mirkin, P. (1982). Valid measurement procedures for continuous evaluation of written expression. *Exceptional Children, 48,* 368–371.

Englert, S., Raphael, T., Fear, K., & Anderson, L. (1988). Students' metacognitive knowledge about how to write informational texts. *Learning Disability Quarterly, 11,* 18–46.

Farr, R., Hughes, C., Robbins, B., & Greene, B. (1990). *What students' writing reveals about their spelling.* Bloomington, IN: Center for Reading and Language Studies.

Fitzgerald, J. (1987). Research on revision in writing. *Review of Educational Research, 57,* 481–506.

Flower, L., & Hayes, J. (1980). The dynamics of composing: Making plans and juggling constraints. In L. Gregg & E. Steinberg (Eds.), *Cognitive processes in writing* (pp. 31–50). Hillsdale, NJ: Lawrence Erlbaum Associates, Inc.

Gentry, R. (1982). An analysis of development spelling in GYNS AT WRK. *Reading Teacher, 36,* 192–200.

Glynn, S., Britton, B., Muth, D., & Dogan, N. (1982). Writing and revising persuasive documents: Cognitive demands. *Journal of Educational Psychology, 74,* 557–567.

Gould, J. (1980). Experiments on composing letters: Some facts, some myths, and some observations. In L. Gregg & E. Steinberg (Eds.), *Cognitive processes in writing* (pp. 97–127). Hillsdale, NJ: Lawrence Erlbaum Associates, Inc.

Graham, S. (1990). The role of production factors in learning disabled students' compositions. *Journal of Educational Psychology, 82,* 781–791.

Graham, S. (1997). Executive control in the revising of students with learning and writing difficulties. *Journal of Educational Psychology, 82,* 781–791.

Graham, S. (1999). Handwriting and spelling instruction for students with learning disabilities: A review. *Learning Disability Quarterly, 22,* 78–98.

Graham, S., Berninger, V., Abbott, R., Abbott, S., & Whitaker, D. (1997). The role of mechanics in composing of elementary school students: A new methodological approach. *Journal of Educational Psychology, 89,* 170–182.

Graham, S., Berninger, V., Weintraub, N., & Schafer, W. (1998). Development of handwriting speed and legibility. *Journal of Educational Research, 92,* 42–51.

Graham, S., & Harris, K. R. (1994a). The effects of whole language on children's writing: A review of literature. *Educational Psychologist, 29,* 187–192.

Graham, S., & Harris, K. R. (1994b). The role and development of self-regulation in the writing process. In D. Schunk & B. Zimmerman (Eds.), *Self-regulation of learning and performance: Issues and educational applications* (pp. 203–228). Hillsdale, NJ: Lawrence Erlbaum Associates, Inc.

Graham, S., & Harris, K. R. (1997a). It can be taught, but it does not develop naturally: Myths and realities in writing instruction. *School Psychology Review, 26,* 414–424.

Graham, S., & Harris, K. R. (1997b). Self-regulation and writing: Where do we go from here? *Contemporary Educational Psychology, 22,* 102–114.

Graham, S., & Harris, K. R. (1997c). Whole language and process writing: Does one approach fit all? In J. Lloyd, E. Kameenui, & D. Chard (Eds.), *Issues in educating students with disabilities* (pp. 239–258). Mahwah, NJ: Lawrence Erlbaum Associates, Inc.

Graham, S., MacArthur, C., & Schwartz, S. (1993). Knowledge of writing and the composing process, attitude towards writing, and self-efficacy for students with and without learning disabilities. *Journal of Learning Disabilities, 26,* 237–249.

Graham, S., MacArthur, C., & Schwartz, S. (1995). Effects of goal setting and procedural facilitation on the revising behavior and writing performance of students with writing and learning problems. *Journal of Educational Psychology, 87,* 230–240.

Graham, S., & Weintraub, N. (1996). A review of handwriting research: Progress and prospects from 1980 to 1994. *Educational Psychology Review, 8,* 7–87.

Harris, K. R., & Graham, S. (1996). *Making the writing process work: Strategies for composition and self-regulation.* Cambridge, MA: Brookline.

Harris, K. R., Graham, S., Reid, R., McElroy, K., & Hamby, R. (1994). Self-monitoring of attention versus self-monitoring of productivity: A cross task comparison. *Learning Disability Quarterly, 17,* 121–139.

Hayes, J. (1996). A new framework for understanding cognition and affect in writing. In M. Levy & S. Ransdell (Eds.), *The science of writing: Theories, methods, individual differences, and applications* (pp. 1–27). Mahwah, NJ: Lawrence Erlbaum Associates, Inc.

Hayes, J., & Flower, L. (1980). Identifying the organization of writing processes. In L. Gregg & E. Steinberg (Eds.), *Cognitive processes in writing* (pp. 3–30). Hillsdale, NJ: Lawrence Erlbaum Associates, Inc.

Hayes, J., & Nash, J. (1996). On the nature of planning in writing. In M. Levy & S. Ransdell (Eds.), *The science of writing: Theories, methods, individual differences, and applications* (pp. 29–55). Mahwah, NJ: Lawrence Erlbaum Associates, Inc.

Henderickson, R. (1994). *The literary life and other curiosities.* New York: Harcourt Brace.

Humes, A. (1983). Research on the composing process. *Review of Educational Research, 53,* 201–216.

Jones, D., & Christensen, C. (1999). The relationship between automaticity in handwriting and students' ability to generate written text. *Journal of Educational Psychology, 91,* 44–49.

Juel, C. (1988). Learning to read and write: A longitudinal study of 54 children from first through fourth grade. *Journal of Educational Psychology, 80,* 437–447.

Kazin, A. (1967). *The Paris Review: Writers at work.* New York: Viking.

Kellogg, R. (1987). Effects of topic knowledge on the allocation of processing time and cognitive effort to writing processes. *Memory & Cognition, 15,* 256–266.

Lamb, B. (1997). *Booknotes: America's finest authors on reading, writing, and the power of ideas.* New York: Random House.

McCutchen, D. (1988). "Functional automaticity" in children's writing: A problem of metacognitive control. *Written Communication, 5,* 306–324.

McCutchen, D. (1995). Cognitive processes in children's writing: Developmental and individual differences. *Issues in Education: Contributions from Educational Psychology, 1,* 123–160.

McCutchen, D. (1996). A capacity theory of writing: Working memory in composition. *Educational Psychology Review, 8,* 299–325.

Page-Voth, V., & Graham, S. (1999). Effects of goal setting and strategy use on the writing performance and self-efficacy of students with writing and learning problems. *Journal of Educational Psychology, 91,* 230–240.

Plimpton, G. (1989). *The writer's chapbook: A compendium of fact, opinion, wit, and advice from the 20th century's preeminent writers.* New York: Viking.

Ransdell, S., & Levy, M. (1996). Working memory constraints on writing quality and fluency. In M. Levy & S. Ransdell (Eds.), *The science of writing: Theories, methods, individual differences, and applications* (pp. 93–106). Mahwah, NJ: Lawrence Erlbaum Associates, Inc.

Reece, J., & Cumming, G. (1996). Evaluating speech-based composition methods: Planning, dictation, and the listening word processor. In M. Levy & S. Ransdell (Eds.), *The science of writing: Theories, methods, individual differences, and applications* (pp. 361–380). Mahwah, NJ: Lawrence Erlbaum Associates, Inc.

Safire, W., & Safire, L. (1992). *Good advice on writing.* New York: Simon & Schuster.

Sawyer, R., Graham, S., & Harris, K. R. (1992). Direct teaching, strategy instruction, and strategy instruction with explicit self-regulation: Effects on learning disabled students' composition skills and self-efficacy. *Journal of Educational Psychology, 84,* 340–352.

Scardamalia, M., & Bereiter, C. (1985). Fostering the development of self-regulation in children's knowledge processing. In S. Chipman, J. Segal, & R. Glaser (Eds.), *Thinking and learning skills: Current research and open questions* (Vol. 2, pp. 563–577). Hillsdale, NJ: Lawrence Erlbaum Associates, Inc.

Scardamalia, M., & Bereiter, C. (1986). Written composition. In M. Wittrock (Ed.), *Handbook of research on teaching* (3rd ed., pp. 778–803). New York: Macmillan.

Schunk, D., & Swartz, C. (1993). Goals and progress feedback: Effects on self-efficacy and writing achievement. *Contemporary Educational Psychology, 18,* 337–354.

Smagorinsky, P. (1987). Graves revisited. *Written Communication, 4,* 331–342.

Smith, C., & Ingersoll, G. (1984). *Written vocabulary of elementary school pupils, ages 6–14.* Bloomington: Indiana University Press.

Troia, G., Graham, S., & Harris, K. J. R. (1999). Teaching students with learning disabilities to mindfully plan when writing. *Exceptional Children, 65,* 253–270.

Varley, J. (1992). *Steel beach.* New York: Ace Books.

Wong, B., Wong, R., & Blenkinsop, J. (1989). Cognitive and metacognitive aspects of learning disabled adolescents' composing problems. *Learning Disability Quarterly, 12,* 300–322.

Zimmerman, B., & Kitsantas, A. (1999). Acquiring writing revision skill: Shifting from process to outcome self-regulatory goals. *Journal of Educational Psychology, 91,* 241–250.

Zimmerman, B., & Riesemberg, R. (1997). Becoming a self-regulated writer: A social cognitive perspective. *Contemporary Educational Psychology, 22,* 73–101.

EDUCATIONAL PSYCHOLOGIST, *35*(1), 13–23
Copyright © 2000, Lawrence Erlbaum Associates, Inc.

Knowledge, Processing, and Working Memory: Implications for a Theory of Writing

Deborah McCutchen

Department of Educational Psychology
University of Washington

This article surveys writing research and attempts to sketch a principled account of how multiple sources of knowledge, stored in long-term memory, are coordinated during writing within the constraints of working memory. The concept of *long-term working memory* is applied to the development of writing expertise. Based on research reviewed, it is speculated that lack of fluent language generation processes constrains novice writers within short-term working memory capacity, whereas fluent encoding and extensive knowledge allow skilled writers to take advantage of long-term memory resources via long-term working memory.

Twenty years ago, Flower and Hayes (1980) offered as a metaphor of the writer the image of a busy switchboard operator who juggles multiple calls, makes connections, and solves problems while presenting an outward voice of composure and control. The metaphor was intended to illustrate the multitask nature of writing and the coordination of knowledge and processing during composition. Hayes and Flower's (1980) metaphor and the cognitive model of writing from which it derives have profoundly influenced psychological studies of writing in the intervening decades. Recently, Hayes (1996) offered a revised model that differs from the 1980 version in several ways, most notably in providing for more articulated sources of knowledge within long-term memory (LTM) and a more explicit role for working memory. Thus, the busy switchboard operator now holds a spot on center stage in the guise of working memory, and contributions of knowledge are explicit. Still lacking, despite the proliferation of writing research over the past 20 years, are detailed descriptions of how knowledge stored in LTM is accessed and used within a limited-capacity working memory.

In this article I attempt to sketch a developmental model of memory and writing processes, one that stresses the interactions between working memory and knowledge stored in LTM, as well as changes in such interactions as writing-relevant knowledge increases. I explore the concept of *long-term working memory* (LT-WM) developed by Ericsson

and Kintsch (1995; Kintsch, 1998) and apply the concept to the development of writing expertise. I begin with a brief discussion of memory theory to provide a context for the discussion of LT-WM, which I then apply to the domain of writing. Although much relevant empirical research remains to be done, I speculate that writing expertise depends on the development of two things: fluent language generation processes and extensive knowledge relevant to writing (e.g., topic knowledge, genre knowledge). The former enable the developing writer to begin to manage the constraints imposed by short-term working memory (ST-WM), whereas the latter allows the writer to move beyond the constraints of ST-WM and take advantage of the resources of the LT-WM.

ST-WM VERSUS LT-WM

Short-term memory (STM) was originally construed as a somewhat static buffer of seven plus or minus two storage units (Miller, 1956). STM contains the contents of consciousness that are the focus of current attention and are thereby distinct from the rest of knowledge stored in LTM. Empirical work by Baddeley (1986, 1998; Baddeley & Hitch, 1974) demonstrated the need for a more dynamic conceptualization of STM, one that Baddeley called *working memory*. Working memory, as described by Baddeley and others (Cantor & Engle, 1993; Daneman & Carpenter, 1980; Just & Carpenter, 1992; Swanson, 1992) incorporates both storage and processing constraints. Trade-offs exist between working memory's storage and processing functions because of resource limitations within the system. When more resources are devoted to

Requests for reprints should be sent to Deborah McCutchen, Educational Psychology, University of Washington, 312 Miller Hall, Box 353600, Seattle, WA 98195–3600. E-mail: mccutch@u.washington.edu

processing, fewer resources are available for storage. Conversely, when storage is privileged, processing can suffer.

Baddeley (1986) defined working memory as "the temporary storage of information that is being processed in any range of cognitive tasks" (p. 43). Kintsch (1998; Ericsson & Kintsch, 1995) argued, however, that the range of cognitive tasks encompassed by such a ST-WM model was limited to the types of arbitrary learning and superficial reasoning tasks that abound in laboratory studies. Such a model of ST-WM, according to Kintsch, could not account for the kinds of extensive reasoning and knowledge manipulation that characterize expertise in real-world cognitive tasks such as chess, medical diagnosis, and comprehension. Kintsch (1998) proposed an alternative account of the working memory employed in such real-world tasks, one he and Ericsson (Ericsson & Kintsch, 1995) called "long-term working memory." LT-WM contains not only the limited number of elements activated in ST-WM, but also retrieval structures that link STM items to related elements in LTM. The items already activated within the capacity-limited STM function as retrieval cues for those parts of LTM to which they connect. Thus, the information available in LT-WM is of two types: those items activated in ST-WM and those items in LTM that can be reached via the retrieval structures. Such LTM elements are not actually stored within working memory, but they can be quickly retrieved when processing requires (in about 400 ms, as estimated by Ericsson & Kintsch, 1995).

Unlike ST-WM, which has strict capacity limitations, the capacity of LT-WM is limited only by the nature of the encoding processes that build retrieval structures and by the extent of knowledge in LTM to which those structures connect. Kintsch (1998) argued that effective retrieval structures result from knowledge that is "strong, stable, well practiced, and automated, so that it can be employed for encoding without additional resource demands" (p. 242) and from encoding processes that are rapid and reliable. Such encoding processes are specific to particular knowledge domains. In the case of comprehension, Kintsch's primary focus, these encoding processes are the normal processes of skilled comprehension (e.g., word recognition, syntactic parsing). In the case of medical expertise, these encoding processes may relate to recognition of diagnostic patterns of symptoms. Thus, the resources of LT-WM are available only in domains of relative expertise. LT-WM is an emergent feature of cognition resulting from an extensive knowledge base and efficient task-specific processing.

From such an LT-WM perspective, the debate about the causal relation between processing and storage capacity in working memory becomes moot (see Ericsson & Kintsch, 1995; Kintsch, 1998). This debate has taken place largely within discussions of reading skill, and proponents of the capacity view argue that less-skilled readers have smaller working memory capacities that then constrain linguistic processes such as lexical access and syntactic parsing (Cantor & Engle, 1993; Just & Carpenter, 1992; Miyake, Just, & Carpenter, 1994; Swanson, 1992). Kintsch reinterpreted such findings, arguing that so-called high span readers simply en code (i.e., comprehend) text more efficiently, build more effective retrieval structures, and thereby store more complete text representations in LTM to be retrieved as needed into LT-WM. Skilled readers thus have access to resources beyond the limits of ST-WM. As Kintsch (1998) explained, "it is not that good readers have a larger box to put things in for temporary storage, but that they are more skilled in putting things into long-term storage and retrieving them again" (pp. 239–240).

Kintsch and Ericsson (1995) argued that traditional working memory descriptions have difficulty accounting for a number of empirical findings, and central in Kintsch's (1998) discussion of comprehension were effects of interrupting comprehension. In a series of studies, Glanzer and his colleagues (Fischer & Glanzer, 1986; Glanzer, Dorfman, & Kaplan, 1981; Glanzer, Fischer, & Dorfman, 1984) compared comprehension of readers who read a normal eight-sentence text with the comprehension of readers who read the same text with unrelated sentences among each of the original eight. According to a traditional ST-WM account, processing the unrelated sentences would displace representations of the developing text from working memory and disrupt comprehension (see, e.g., the STM processing description in the model of Kintsch & van Dijk, 1978). In Glanzer's experiments, however, interruptions had no effect on comprehension, and the only effect was an increased reading time of approximately 400 ms after each interruption. By an LT-WM account, after each interruption, processing of the next related sentence provides cues to representations of prior text stored in LTM. A coherent text representation develops within LT-WM as retrieval structures (capitalizing on LTM knowledge of topic and text structures) provide ready access to previous text representations and link them to text elements currently being processed. Furthermore, just as LT-WM theory would predict, processing times were found to be longer still when the interrupted texts contained unfamiliar content and followed the format of technical reports (McNamara & Kintsch, 1996), thereby reducing the usefulness of LTM topic and genre knowledge.

WRITING ACQUISITION: KNOWLEDGE, PROCESSING, AND LT-WM

Working memory (most frequently cast within a more traditional ST-WM framework) has received considerable recent attention from writing researchers (Butterfield, Hacker, & Albertson, 1996; Kellogg, 1987, 1996; Levy & Ransdell, 1995; McCutchen, 1996; Ransdell & Levy, 1996). Writing research is replete with examples of process interactions and recursions, all of which must be orchestrated within some executive system. For example, data as diverse as protocols (Flower & Hayes, 1980, 1981, 1984; Hayes & Flower, 1980;

McCutchen, 1984, 1988), pause times (Matsuhashi, 1982), and keystrokes (Levy & Ransdell, 1995) indicate that skilled writers continually juggle knowledge and process.

This view of skilled writing, however, is quite at odds with the portrait of novice writers painted most vividly by Bereiter and Scardamalia (1987). For the novice, writing is less a juggling act and more a matter of simply getting ideas down on paper as they are retrieved from LTM. Such a streamlined process is the heart of the knowledge-telling strategy described by Bereiter and Scardamalia. Based on their observations of children's writing, Bereiter and Scardamalia inferred a writing process cued not by rich knowledge sources, but by the previous sentence or the writing prompt.

A theory of writing development should entail a principled account of how the novice writer gains expertise and should include an explanation of how multiple sources of knowledge, stored in LTM, are coordinated and used in various writing processes within the limits of a constrained working memory. The distinction between ST-WM and LT-WM provides the beginning of such a developmental account. I suggest that novice writers are indeed constrained by working memory limitations. Because they lack fluent text-generation processes and extensive writing-relevant knowledge, children are unable to deal with the multiple demands imposed by the writing processes described by Hayes and Flower (1980). Young writers, and less sophisticated writers in general (Daiute, 1981, 1984; Flower, 1979), are constrained by the limitations of ST-WM and therefore depend on alternative writing strategies, such as knowledge telling.

In contrast, skilled writers[1] possess fluent text-generation and transcription processes, as well as extensive knowledge about topics, text genre, and routines for coordinating writing processes. Such an assertion is much in line with the arguments put forth by Graham and Harris (2000) concerning the role of self-regulation and transcription skills in writing development. I wish to add to their argument a further assertion that such fluent encoding processes and rich knowledge bases enable skilled writers to move beyond the limits of ST-WM and capitalize on the resources of LT-WM.

NOVICE WRITERS AND ST-WM CONSTRAINTS

There exists abundant evidence that novice writers, especially young novices, are severely constrained by their lack of fluent encoding processes during writing (see Graham, Berninger, Abbott, Abbott, & Whitaker, 1997; Graham & Harris, 2000; McCutchen, 1996). I survey such research

only briefly and relate it, when possible, to working memory issues. Such lower level skills, identified as transcription and text generation by Berninger and Swanson (1994), constitute the translating process described in the original Hayes and Flower (1980) model. Text generation is assumed to share many components with oral language generation, such as content selection, lexical retrieval, and syntactic processes. In contrast, transcription entails the cognitive and physical acts of forming *written* (as opposed to *spoken*) representations of text.

Transcription processes (notably spelling and handwriting) seem most limiting in the earliest stages of writing acquisition. For example, King and Rentel (1981) found clear quality and quantity differences favoring dictation over writing (i.e., text generation without vs. with added transcription demands) in a study of first- and second-grade children. Differences favoring dictation are more qualified for older children, however (Bereiter & Scardamalia, 1987; McCutchen, 1987). Bourdin and Fayol (1994) examined transcription processes within the explicit context of working memory. They varied response modality (spoken vs. written) in a serial recall task and found that recall was significantly poorer in the written condition for children but not for adults. They interpreted these findings as evidence that the transcription process of adults, but not children, was sufficiently fluent to operate with minimal working memory demands. Bourdin and Fayol then required adults to write in cursive uppercase letters, thereby preventing use of their overlearned, highly fluent transcription processes (and, I suggest, depriving them of access to LT-WM). In this condition, adults (when constrained by the limits of ST-WM) also showed poorer recall when writing. In a related series of experiments, Bourdin and Fayol (1993) changed the task from serial recall to sentence generation and again demonstrated that transcription imposed resource costs for children but not for adults. Thus, until transcription processes develop sufficient fluency, writers seem constrained by ST-WM limits.

Working memory has also been related to text generation and writing skill in a number of other tasks. Bereiter and Scardamalia (1987) found that children's ability to defend a thesis in an essay was related to the number of informational chunks they could coordinate within a single sentence (a combined span and text-generation task). Tetroe (1984; reported in Bereiter & Scardamalia, 1987) independently assessed children's working memory spans and examined each child's ability to honor multiple ending-sentence constraints. Tetroe saw a marked decrease in children's ability to honor ending-sentence constraints as the number of constraints exceeded the child's memory span. Similarly, McCutchen and Perfetti (1982) observed developmental differences in children's ability to honor multiple constraints in a writing task and explicitly modeled those differences in a computer simulation that varied the amount of information in working memory during each text-generation cycle. We argued that as children's

---

[1]In this context I use the terms *skilled writer* and *expert writer* interchangeably to denote the level of skill possessed by literate adults who express themselves well in writing. I do not reserve the term *expert* for such literary artists as described by Graham and Harris (2000).

language encoding developed fluency with age (an assumption supported by our finding that older children wrote both longer and more coherent texts), they were increasingly able to handle the memory requirements imposed by our writing task. Taken together, such studies support the importance of fluent text-generation processes in writing and suggest that without fluency writers cannot move beyond ST-WM limitations.

Although LT-WM was not explicitly discussed, McCutchen, Covill, Hoyne, and Mildes (1994) documented relations among text-generation processes, working memory, writing skill, and LTM knowledge. In that study, elementary and middle-school students wrote essays and participated in two working memory tasks, a reading span task, in which students read lists of sentences and recalled the final word in each sentence, and a speaking span task, in which students generated a sentence for each word on lists and recalled the words. Half of the students had no further task constraints; that is, they read and were free to generate sentences that were unrelated to one another. However, we imposed an additional discourse constraint on the remaining students, asking these students to read and generate brief stories. Thus, in the story condition, we permitted students to use their knowledge of narrative structures (stored in LTM) to augment their performance in the working memory task.

With no discourse constraints, we found that only speaking span correlated with writing skill. That is, without the benefit of LTM knowledge of narrative structures, fluency of text-generation processes (not text-comprehension processes) predicted writing skill. Under story constraints, however, both speaking span and reading span correlated significantly with writing skill, suggesting that better writers' access to narrative structures in LTM improved their performance in both the reading and the speaking span tasks. Most interesting, only the more skilled writers in the sample showed improved memory spans in the story condition. From an LT-WM perspective, these findings suggest that only the more skilled writers, with their more fluent text-generation processes, were able to use their narrative knowledge to tap LT-WM resources. Without fluent language encoding processes, the less-skilled writers remained constrained by ST-WM.

In the same study, we also examined the processing assumption more directly and documented that more skilled writers indeed process individual words more fluently. Using a lexical decision task, we found that skilled writers were both more rapid and more accurate in accessing individual words in memory. Additional evidence came from an analysis of the children's essays. Sentences written by skilled writers were longer than those by less-skilled writers, again suggesting more developed text-generation processes. Thus, the analysis of children's texts supported our interpretation of the memory data—skilled writers showed evidence of more fluent language encoding processes that

enabled them to better cope with working memory constraints.

I recently reexamined the link between writing skill and encoding fluency, specifically transcription fluency (e.g., handwriting and spelling) in a study of first- and second-grade writers (McCutchen et al., in press). Children completed a battery of reading and writing assessments, as well as a composition task that was scored for overall narrative quality. I reasoned that inefficient handwriting processes should increase ST-WM demands during composing (see Bourdin & Fayol, 1994) and limit text quality. Similarly, if words' spellings were not stored as easily retrievable LTM knowledge, the construction of spellings online would also increase processing load and decrease text quality. In a regression analysis, reported here for the first time, I found that three transcription variables—number of sentences produced and speed of forming letters (two fluency measures) and spelling knowledge—combined to account for a significant portion of the variance in writing quality ($R^2 = .61$). Such findings replicate previous research (Berninger & Swanson, 1994) and suggest that fluent encoding processes improve the performance of novice writers when constrained by ST-WM and in some conditions (e.g., the story condition of McCutchen et al., 1994) help writers gain access to additional LT-WM resources.

Lack of fluency in language encoding processes is not confined to young writers. Relations between language encoding processes and writing skill have been reported for high school as well as college students (Benton, Kraft, Glover, & Plake, 1984). Older writers who lack fluency (sometimes referred to as "basic writers" in composition research) may continue to be constrained by ST-WM limitations. Daiute (1981, 1984) suggested that memory limitations make it difficult for basic writers to avoid (and later correct) certain grammatical errors, such as subject–verb agreement, because such structures become more difficult to coordinate as more words intervene between key constituents. She supported her assertion by documenting negative correlations between memory capacity (as measured by sentence recall) and the occurrence of errors in students' texts. In addition, Fayol, Largy, and Lemaire (1994) were able to experimentally induce subject–verb agreement errors by increasing their participants' memory load during a writing task, thereby documenting a causal rather than merely correlational link between ST-WM resource demands and writing outcomes.

If access to LT-WM resources depends on fluent task-specific encoding processes, as Kintsch (1998; Ericsson & Kintsch, 1995) argued, then one would predict that writers would be confined to ST-WM resources until encoding processes specific to writing, such as transcription and text generation, become sufficiently fluent. Only with fluent encoding processes can writers begin to build retrieval structures to information stored in LTM and, when such LTM knowledge is itself sufficiently rich, capitalize on the resources of LT-WM.

SKILLED WRITERS AND LT-WM

Is there evidence to support the claim that skilled writers use LT-WM resources, as Kintsch (1998) argued skilled readers do? To date, no writing research has explicitly used the LT-WM framework, but much of the writing research involving working memory and writing-relevant knowledge is consistent with predictions derived from such a framework.

In seminal work, Kellogg (1987, see also 1996) investigated general issues of working memory demands in writing. He was most interested in comparing the processing demands of the various subprocesses of writing, and he trained college students to distinguish their planning, translating, and reviewing processes. He then asked students to write essays, periodically probing them as to the process in which they were currently engaged. Although Kellogg found that translating (i.e., language encoding processes) sometimes demanded fewer resources than planning and reviewing, he concluded that none of the processes pushed writers near capacity limits. According to an LT-WM account, the college writers that Kellogg studied were readily able to encode representations of their developing texts into LTM and use the expanded resources of LT-WM. Such text representations in LTM probably also helped Kellogg's writers move between the probe and writing tasks, much as Kintsch (1998) suggested readers used LT-WM when interrupted during comprehension.

Levy and Ransdell (1995) also examined resource demands in skilled writers and argued that resource demands do not necessarily decrease for skilled writers, as may be expected if ST-WM resources were the only working memory resources involved in writing (see also Glynn, Britton, Muth, & Dugan, 1982). The fluency of language encoding processes of skilled writers should, according to traditional working memory accounts, reduce the overall processing demands in ST-WM. In their study, however, Levy and Ransdell (1995) focused not only on encoding processes but on the overall combination of knowledge and processing that skilled writers bring to the writing task. We may speculate that their skilled writers employed LT-WM as well as ST-WM resources. As their writers coordinated rhetorical forms, organized topic knowledge, and so on, they set for themselves a more demanding writing task and may well have devoted as much overall effort to composing as less-skilled writers. The key difference may be that the fluency of skilled writers' encoding processes and the accessibility of their writing-relevant knowledge shifted the locus of processing from ST-WM to LT-WM, resulting in better writing, if not lower resource demands overall.

Ransdell and Levy (1996) introduced the variable of individual differences (in reading skill) into their working memory task as they manipulated storage and processing demands. Ransdell and Levy asked participants to hold words in memory (the storage demand) while writing a sentence for each word (the simultaneous processing demand). In addition, Ransdell and Levy stressed word recall in one condition, thereby privileging storage, and stressed sentence complexity in another condition, thereby privileging processing. They found that the most skilled readers in the study could indeed allocate resources according to task demands, recalling more words when memory was stressed and generating more complex sentences when processing was stressed; but readers of lower skill were less flexible. An LT-WM interpretation of such individual differences would hold that the more efficient language processes and richer linguistic knowledge of the skilled readers enabled them to generate more complex sentences and better utilize LT-WM to meet the memory demands of the task.

THE ROLE OF KNOWLEDGE IN LT-WM

Thus, there is abundant evidence that general processes of language encoding (specifically, transcription and text generation) become more fluent with age and with the reading and writing experiences that generally come with age. However, according to Kintsch (1998), LT-WM depends on both efficient encoding processes and rich task-specific knowledge. Is there comparable research documenting relations between LTM knowledge and the development of writing skill? I focus here on two types of knowledge that have been the focus of considerable research: genre and topic knowledge.

Genre Knowledge

Familiarity with a genre can theoretically influence writing by providing access to an organized schema in LTM, and when writers can employ the resources of LT-WM, they are able to use such knowledge to assist ongoing processing. The protocol of one expert writer, a wine columnist for a large metropolitan newspaper (McCutchen, 1984), clearly revealed his genre knowledge in his detailed vision for the structural features of his column:

> The general structure has got to be, we've got to give them some information about Chateau Latour, make it kind of real to them, give them something to chew on, and then we've got to go through the tasting notes because we had a tasting of Chateau Latour from 1924 to 1967, which means that you have to save enough space to write about, you know, the wines themselves. But [first] we've got to say something about Chateau Latour. (p. 228)

Issues of genre also extend into writers' broader knowledge of the disciplinary community for whom (or perhaps more appropriately *with* whom) they write. For example, writers generally learn the discourse forms and honor the rhetorical values of their respective academic disciplines

(MacDonald, 1992; Myers, 1985; Stockton, 1995). Skilled writers seem to have ready access to, if not explicit awareness of, such rhetorical knowledge (Langer, 1992; Stockton, 1995). This ready access is evidenced by the fact that genre and stylistic knowledge seem to influence many other processes, including even lexical and syntactic choices (Barton, 1995; Bazerman, 1984; MacDonald, 1992; Vande Kopple, 1998).

In a recent study, McCutchen, Francis, and Kerr (1997) observed marked differences in access to genre knowledge by students with different levels of writing skill. We recorded protocols as middle-school students collaboratively revised texts in which we had planted both spelling and meaning errors. Skilled writers quickly developed a macrostructure of the text (Kintsch, 1998; Kintsch & van Dijk, 1978), reflecting their knowledge of the essay genre. Even during their initial reading, skilled writers recognized concluding statements that appeared in the introductions, noting these errors with comments such as "That shouldn't be there either 'cause it's too fast."

In contrast, less-skilled writers paid little attention to discourse-level features. They examined sentences individually and rarely considered the global structure of the text. Such a strategy made it particularly difficult for them to detect errors involving meaning (as opposed to spelling). The following excerpt is illustrative of the sentence-by-sentence strategy. Italics are added to highlight the student's evaluative statements.

> (reading) "Christopher Columbus was determined to find an all water route to the East Indies … East Indies." *That's good.* (reading) "Discovering this could bring him fame and fortune. However, however, Columbus also believed that the world was round." *OK.* (reading) "Many people"—*geez!* (corrects spelling, then reads) "laughed at this idea. They thought the world was flat." *Next, that's good.* (reading) "But still the sailors threatened to take over and turn, take over and turn back." *That's good.* (p. 673)

Thus, skilled writers seem to access a macrostructure for the text on which they are working, and such macrostructures are derived from their general knowledge of text structures, or genres. Extensive knowledge of a genre enables skilled writers to take advantage of LT-WM by building retrieval structures from the relatively small number of activated text elements in ST-WM to a more extensive, elaborated text representation stored in LTM. In our study, skilled writers therefore recognized when a text sentence was out of place (e.g., when an opening sentence, processed within ST-WM, links to the *Conclusion* slot of the essay schema in LTM). Lacking extensive genre knowledge[2]

to enable LT-WM, less-skilled writers were constrained by the limits of ST-WM and forced to attend to one sentence at a time.

Existing research provides considerable evidence for developmental differences in genre knowledge and for links between genre knowledge and writing skill, even for children. Due largely to children's broad early experience with narratives at home and at school (Durkin, 1978–1979; Sulzby & Teale, 1987), very young children show signs of emergent narrative schemas (Brown, 1976; Stein & Glenn, 1979; Sulzby, 1985). Fitzgerald and Teasley (1986) provided evidence for a causal link between genre knowledge and writing skill, demonstrating that the quality of children's written stories improved after instruction in narrative structure. Children's knowledge of expository genres generally develops later (Englert, Stewart, & Hiebert, 1988; Langer, 1986), and comparisons reveal that children's written narratives are generally superior to their expositions (e.g., Cox, Shanahan, & Tinzmann, 1991; Hidi & Hildyard, 1983; but see Langer, 1986, as well as McCutchen, 1987, for qualifications). The difference in genre familiarity is apparent to children themselves, and they claim to be better at writing narratives than essays (Bereiter & Scardamalia, 1987). Even children with writing disabilities, for whom transcription processes exert considerable processing demands, produced spoken and written narratives that were similar in quality (Montague, Graves, & Leavell, 1991), whereas with essays, the written texts of children with writing disabilities were both shorter and lower in quality than spoken texts (Graham, 1990).

According to an LT-WM interpretation, access to rich knowledge of a particular genre enables writers to utilize the resources of LT-WM, building retrieval structures between text elements currently processed in ST-WM and organized text representations within LTM. However, children's writing may also benefit from genre knowledge even before their encoding processes are sufficiently fluent to support LT-WM. Children's use of genre knowledge may be more implicit, still operating within the constraints of ST-WM. According to Bereiter and Scardamalia (1987), the knowledge-telling strategy uses cues from the assignment (genre and topic cues) to formulate memory probes. When children are more familiar with a genre, the memory probes generated as part of the knowledge-telling process will be more systematically related and should result in retrieval of more coherent content. Thus, even though children may not have access to LT-WM, as expert writers do, children's genre knowledge may influence their writing because it is incorporated within knowledge-telling operations in ST-WM. We may predict, however, that retrieval times initiated by knowledge telling may differ from the 400 ms retrieval times associated with LT-WM processes, but such studies remain to be done.

---

[2]I am not suggesting that less-skilled writers have no knowledge of genre. Kintsch (1998) argued, however, that knowledge must be extensive, stable, and well practiced before it can be used to support the operation of LT-WM.

Topic Knowledge

Considerable research documents a substantial role for topic knowledge in a range of tasks, including reading and writing. Topic expertise has marked effects on readers' approaches to texts (Peskin, 1998; Spilich, Vesonder, Chiesi, & Voss, 1979; Voss, Vesonder, & Spilich, 1980; Wineburg, 1991). Even for young children, extensive topic knowledge increases the sophistication of cognitive processing in a variety of reasoning tasks (e.g., Chi, 1976; Means & Voss, 1985).

Instructional researchers have long argued that topic knowledge should improve writing (Calkins, 1986), and writing research supports that claim. Bereiter and Scardamalia (1987) observed that children generated more content during planning about familiar topics, compared with unfamiliar topics.[3] In a study of students from fourth, sixth, and eighth grades, I found that writers who were more knowledgeable about their topic wrote better texts than did writers who were less knowledgeable (McCutchen, 1986; see also Langer, 1984). Football texts written by football experts were both more coherent and more deeply elaborated than those written by nonexperts. In a subsequent analysis of data collected as the children planned, I also found that football experts produced longer plans than nonexperts.

DeGroff (1987) linked topic knowledge (of baseball) to the quality of children's first drafts, as well as to their revision. Topic knowledge was especially important in children's ability to specify the nature of text problems during conferencing. In addition, Butterfield, Hacker, and Plumb (1994) extended such findings to adult writers, documenting a positive relation between adults' topic knowledge (cricket and meteorology) and their revising effectiveness.

I also examined the effects of topic knowledge in the revision study discussed previously (McCutchen et al., 1997). Participants revised two texts, one about Christopher Columbus (a familiar topic) and another about Margaret Mead (an unfamiliar topic). In that study, both adults and middle-school students were more likely to detect and correct meaning-related problems in the Columbus text than in the Mead text. Topic knowledge, however, did not influence the correction of spelling errors.

An LT-WM analysis can elegantly account for such findings. Evaluation of the spellings of individual words required processing that was well within the constraints of ST-WM for these writers. Writers either noticed misspelling and automatically retrieved the correct alternatives, or they did not notice misspellings; but in both cases, knowledge of the text topic was irrelevant. However, to detect logical inconsistencies in meaning that spanned multiple sentences, writers needed to draw on the resources of LT-WM. Writers were better able to build effective retrieval structures to other relevant knowledge in LTM when the texts described a familiar topic (the voyage of Columbus). Thus, when revising the familiar text, writers had ready access (within 400 ms) to extensive topic knowledge that helped them detect and correct logical problems in text meaning. Lacking such extensive knowledge about Margaret Mead's work in Samoa, writers were less able to use LT-WM resources to relate elements across multiple sentences and paragraphs.

A further example of a skilled writer's use of topic knowledge can be found in a later excerpt from the protocol of the wine columnist (McCutchen, 1994). Early in his protocol he described his newspaper audience, an audience not necessarily expert about wines. Later, in the midst of a detailed description of the cabernet sauvignon grape, he interrupted his writing and said, "Now I should say 'esters and aldehydes,' but if I did that, then I'd have to explain about esters and aldehydes … Why not just talk about smells and flavors?" (p. 5). His deft change of focus (from the chemical basis of wine to its perceptual qualities) revealed that, even at the point of word choice, he was readily able to access related information in LTM to communicate better with his audience.

Like genre knowledge, topic knowledge may also benefit young writers even before they have access to LT-WM resources. During knowledge telling, topic cues are theoretically used to generate memory probes, in much the same way as genre cues are used (Bereiter & Scardamalia, 1987). Thus, writers who use the knowledge-telling strategy should also produce better texts when they are more familiar with a topic, not because they have access to LT-WM, but simply because the knowledge accessed by ST-WM probes is more interconnected. Even knowledge telling can thereby produce relatively coherent texts when its associative search processes operate on a rich and well-structured knowledge base. Again, however, we may predict differences in retrieval times associated with knowledge-telling versus LT-WM processes.

Berninger, Fuller, and Whitaker (1996) documented a clear link between knowledge and writing strategy in a study of graduate students working in a novel domain. Berninger et al. collected protocols as trainees in a school psychology program wrote case reports, and they saw these relatively skilled writers resort to a linear writing process much like knowledge telling. As the trainees struggled to coordinate newly acquired knowledge with a novel genre, many relied on the writing assignment to prompt step-by-step retrieval of relevant content, rather than on a global diagnosis fine-tuned to the specifics of each case.[4]

---

[3]Bereiter and Scardamalia (1987) found no quality differences, however, between the texts children wrote on familiar and unfamiliar topics. They asked children to suggest their own topics and thereby perhaps limited the extent to which the unfamiliar topics were truly unfamiliar. When familiarity has been assessed independently, rather than by the children themselves, differences in text quality consistently emerge (DeGroff, 1987; Langer, 1984; McCutchen, 1986).

---

[4]Kintsch (1998) described studies of text recall in which medical interns showed similar reliance on a more surface-level textbase, in contrast to experienced doctors who employed knowledge-dependent situation models.

Thus, without the benefit of deep topic knowledge and a familiar genre, skilled writers can lose access to LT-WM resources and resort to less mature strategies to cope with writing demands.

Of course, knowledge of topic and genre are not the only sources of knowledge that distinguish skilled from novice writers. Unlike the acute sense of audience that guided the wine columnist's word choice, attention to readers' needs are frequently lacking in the texts of less-skilled writers. Although children have been observed to make allowances for an absent listener (Littleton, 1998) and modify their arguments for different audiences (Cameron, Hunt, & Linton, 1996), their texts are not always reader-friendly and often contain ambiguous references and other textual infelicities (Bartlett, 1982; Beal, 1996). Flower (1979) described similar problems in the writing of older novice writers. In addition, students with writing disabilities (as well as young children) seem to lack the metacognitive, self-regulatory processes possessed by skilled writers (Beal, 1996; Englert, Raphael, Anderson, Gregg, & Anthony, 1989; Graham & Harris, 2000). Considerable research remains to be done to examine the implications of such knowledge for a theory of LT-WM in writing.

THE WORKING MEMORY PARADOX

Writing researchers interested in working memory, including myself (McCutchen, 1996; McCutchen et al., 1994), have often made the general claim that more fluent language generation processes free working memory resources and allow for higher level processes such as planning and reviewing. Details of the interactions of such processes within working memory have, however, remained sketchy. Such lack of specificity in our theories has led to something of a paradox in our attempts to wed traditional working memory theory and data: Less-skilled writers sometimes show more fluency generating text than do skilled writers.

Protocols of skilled writers (Flower & Hayes, 1980, 1981, 1984; Hayes & Flower, 1980; McCutchen, 1984, 1988) often reveal their hard work as they wrestle with ideas and language—the juggling act described by Flower and Hayes (1980)—whereas less sophisticated writers often jump straightaway into producing text with what looks like surprising ease. In fact, children are frequently incredulous when told that some writers think for 15 min or more before they write anything, and young writers often begin producing text within a minute of receiving an assignment (Bereiter & Scardamalia, 1987).

Contrast, for example, the protocol of the wine columnist as he began his weekly column (from McCutchen, 1994) with that of a second grader writing about her favorite activity (McCutchen, 1988). Before he wrote a word, the wine columnist laid out requirements for his opening sentence:

Alright, so now you need a lead-in sentence and it's got to be something that's going to 1) catch the audience's eye, 2) given the way I usually write the column, it's got to be reasonably ornate, and 3) it's got to have something to do with the goddamn topic. (p. 4)

The protocol of the second grader, however, consisted largely of her saying aloud the words as she wrote them. She said aloud, "My dad can swim better than us all," as she wrote *My dad is the swimmer.* She said, "Sometimes my brother tries to dunk me" as she wrote *Sometimes my brother dunk's* [sic] *me.* She said, "My mom makes me swim back and forth ten times" as she wrote *My mother make's* [sic] *me swim back and forth over and over.* Her protocol revealed the knowledge-telling strategy in full swing, and somewhat paradoxically, her writing progressed more fluently than that of the wine columnist.

The solution to this apparent paradox is also evident in the protocol excerpts. The second grader did indeed generate text relatively easily within the constraints of ST-WM using her knowledge-telling strategy. Whereas text generation was the primary task the young writer set for herself, the wine columnist imposed task constraints reflecting his sense of genre, audience, style, and topic. That is, the wine columnist accessed a wide range of knowledge stored in LTM as he composed, and the constraints imposed by that knowledge complicated his writing task considerably. Still, such complications did not exceed his working memory capacity because he possessed two crucial components of writing expertise—fluent language encoding processes and extensive writing-relevant knowledge. The skilled writer was thereby able to transcend the limits of ST-WM and capitalize on the resources of LT-WM. The result was not necessarily an effortless writing process, but an effective one that yielded high-quality text.

CONCLUSIONS

I have used this review to explore implications of a theory of LT-WM (Ericsson & Kintsch, 1995; Kintsch, 1998) within the development of writing expertise. According to such theory, emerging fluency in language encoding processes enables developing writers to begin to manage constraints imposed by ST-WM; but without considerable processing fluency and extensive writing-relevant knowledge, novice writers remain limited by ST-WM capacity. Within such constraints, writing strategies such as knowledge telling may serve an adaptive function. Because knowledge telling merges content retrieval with text generation and results in actual words on the page, it gets the job done in many writing situations, and it does so within the limits of ST-WM.

Once language encoding processes become sufficiently fluent and knowledge bases sufficiently rich, writers can transcend the processing limits of ST-WM and capitalize on

LT-WM. Like beginning writers, skilled writers use ST-WM resources to construct the sentences that comprise their texts. However, their fluent sentence-generation processes, combined with their rich knowledge bases, enable skilled writers to link developing sentences to extensive knowledge stored in LTM. Their sentence constructions (including word choice, syntax, and semantic intent) can therefore be influenced by earlier text choices (stored in an LTM text representation), by structural constraints for the chosen genre, by knowledge about a specific audience, and by knowledge about the general topic. However, access to and coordination of these multiple sources of LTM knowledge become possible only when processing shifts from ST-WM to LT-WM.

I have sketched how LT-WM may contribute to writing expertise in only the broadest of strokes. Much empirical research needs to be done to fill in details and to evaluate specific theoretical predictions. For example, can we use response-time methodologies to distinguish knowledge-telling processes from LT-WM processes? Can we develop experimental situations that deny skilled writers access to LT-WM resources and systematically induce less mature writing? With a better specified model of working memory in writing, one that distinguishes LT-WM from ST-WM, we may begin to answer such questions.

ACKNOWLEDGMENTS

Preparation of this article and research reported herein were supported by Center Grant P50HD 33812 and Grant HD–26349 from the National Institute of Child Health and Human Development.

REFERENCES

Baddeley, A. D. (1986). *Working-memory.* New York: Oxford University Press.

Baddeley, A. D. (1998). *Human memory: Theory and practice.* Boston: Allyn & Bacon.

Baddeley, A. D., & Hitch, G. (1974). Working memory. In G. A. Bower (Ed.), *Recent advances in learning and motivation* (Vol. 8, pp. 47–89). New York: Academic.

Bartlett, E. J. (1982). Learning to revise. In M. Nystrand (Ed.), *What writers know: The language, process, and structure of written texts* (pp. 345–363). New York: Academic.

Barton, E. L. (1995). Contrastive and non-contrastive connectives: Metadiscourse functions in argumentation. *Written Communication, 12,* 219–239.

Bazerman, C. (1984). Modern evolution of the experimental report in physics: Spectroscopic articles in *Physical Review,* 1893–1980. *Social Studies of Science, 14,* 163–196.

Beal, C. R. (1996). The role of comprehension monitoring in children's revision. *Educational Psychology Review, 8,* 219–238.

Benton, S. L., Kraft, R. G., Glover, J. A., & Plake, B. S. (1984). Cognitive capacity differences among writers. *Journal of Educational Psychology, 76,* 820–834.

Bereiter, C., & Scardamalia, M. (1987). *The psychology of written composition.* Hillsdale, NJ: Lawrence Erlbaum Associates, Inc.

Berninger, V. W., Fuller, F., & Whitaker, D. (1996). A process model of writing development across the life span. *Educational Psychology Review, 8,* 193–218.

Berninger, V. W., & Swanson, H. L. (1994). Modifying Hayes and Flower's model of skilled writing to explain beginning and developing writing. In J. S. Carlson (Series Ed.) & E. C. Butterfield (Vol. Ed.), *Advances in cognition and educational practice: Vol. 2. Children's writing: Toward a process theory of the development of skilled writing* (pp. 57–81). Greenwich, CT: JAI.

Bourdin, B., & Fayol, M. (1993, August). *Comparing speaking span and writing span: A working memory approach.* Paper presented at the meeting of the European Association for Research in Learning and Instruction, Aix-en-Provence, France.

Bourdin, B., & Fayol, M. (1994). Is written language production more difficult than oral language production? A working memory approach. *International Journal of Psychology, 29,* 591–620.

Brown, A. L. (1976). The construction of temporal succession by preoperational children. In A. D. Pick (Ed.), *Minnesota symposium on child psychology* (Vol. 10, pp. 28–83). Minneapolis: University of Minnesota Press.

Butterfield, E. C., Hacker, D. J., & Albertson, L. (1996). Environmental, cognitive, and metacognitive processes underlying text revision. *Educational Psychology Review, 8,* 259–297.

Butterfield, E. C., Hacker, D. J., & Plumb, C. (1994). Topic knowledge, linguistic knowledge, and revision skill as determinants of text revision. In J. S. Carlson (Series Ed.) & E. C. Butterfield (Vol. Ed.), *Advances in cognition and educational practice: Vol. 2. Children's writing: Toward a process theory of the development of skilled writing* (pp. 83–141). Greenwich, CT: JAI.

Calkins, L. M. (1986). *The art of teaching writing.* Portsmouth, NH: Heinemann.

Cameron, C. A., Hunt, A. K., & Linton, M. (1996). Written expression in the primary classroom: Children write in social time. *Educational Psychology Review, 8,* 125–150.

Cantor, J., & Engle, R. W. (1993). Working memory capacity as long-term memory activation: An individual difference approach. *Journal of Experimental Psychology: Learning, Memory, and Cognition, 19,* 1101–1114.

Chi, M. T. H. (1976). Short-term memory limitations in children: Capacity or processing deficits? *Memory & Cognition, 4,* 559–572.

Cox, B. E., Shanahan, T., & Tinzmann, M. B. (1991). Children's knowledge of organization, cohesion, and voice in written exposition. *Research in the Teaching of English, 25,* 179–218.

Daiute, C. A. (1981). Psycholinguistic foundations of the writing process. *Research in the Teaching of English, 15,* 5–22.

Daiute, C. A. (1984). Performance limits on writers. In R. Beach & L. S. Bridwell (Eds.), *New directions in composition research* (pp. 205–224). New York: Guilford.

Daneman, M., & Carpenter, P. A. (1980). Individual differences in working memory and reading. *Journal of Verbal Learning and Verbal Behavior, 19,* 450–466.

DeGroff, L. C. (1987). The influence of prior knowledge on writing, conferencing, and revising. *The Elementary School Journal, 88,* 105–116.

Durkin, D. (1978–1979). What classroom observations reveal about reading comprehension instruction. *Reading Research Quarterly, 14,* 481–533.

Englert, C. S, Raphael, T., Anderson, L., Gregg, S., & Anthony, H. (1989). Exposition: Reading, writing, and the metacognitive knowledge of learning disabled students. *Learning Disabilities Research, 5,* 5–24.

Englert, C. S., Stewart, S. R., & Hiebert, E. H. (1988). Young writers' use of text structure in expository text generation. *Journal of Educational Psychology, 80,* 143–151.

Ericsson, K. A., & Kintsch, W. (1995). Long-term working memory. *Psychological Review, 102,* 211–245.

Fayol, M., Largy, P., & Lemaire, P. (1994). Cognitive overload and orthographic errors: When cognitive overload enhances subject–verb agreement, a study in French written language. *Quarterly Journal of Experimental Psychology, 47,* 437–464.

Fischer, B., & Glanzer, M. (1986). Short-term storage and the processing of cohesion during reading. *Quarterly Journal of Experimental Psychology, 38,* 431–460.

Fitzgerald, J., & Teasley, A. B. (1986). Effects of instruction in narrative structure on children's writing. *Journal of Educational Psychology, 78,* 424–432.

Flower, L. S. (1979). Writer-based prose: A cognitive basis for problems in writing. *College English, 41,* 19–37.

Flower, L. S., & Hayes, J. R. (1980). The dynamics of composing: Making plans and juggling constraints. In L. W. Gregg & E. R. Steinberg (Eds.), *Cognitive processes in writing* (pp. 31–50). Hillsdale, NJ: Lawrence Erlbaum Associates, Inc.

Flower, L. S., & Hayes, J. R. (1981). Plans that guide the composing process. In C. H. Frederiksen & J. F. Dominic (Eds.), *Writing: The nature, development, and teaching of written communication* (Vol. 2, pp. 39–58). Hillsdale, NJ: Lawrence Erlbaum Associates, Inc.

Flower, L. S., & Hayes, J. R. (1984). Images, plans, and prose: The representation of meaning in writing. *Written Communication, 1,* 120–160.

Glanzer, M., Dorfman, D., & Kaplan, B. (1981). Short-term storage in the processing of text. *Journal of Verbal Learning and Verbal Behavior, 20,* 656–670.

Glanzer, M., Fischer, B., & Dorfman, D. (1984). Short-term storage in reading. *Journal of Verbal Learning and Verbal Behavior, 23,* 467–486.

Glynn, S. M., Britton, B. K., Muth, D., & Dugan, N. (1982). Writing and revising persuasive documents: Cognitive demands. *Journal of Educational Psychology, 74,* 557–567.

Graham, S. (1990). The role of production factors in learning disabled students' compositions. *Journal of Educational Psychology, 82,* 781–791.

Graham, S., Berninger, V. W., Abbott, R. D., Abbott, S., & Whitaker, D. (1997). The role of mechanics in composing of elementary school students: A new methodological approach. *Journal of Educational Psychology, 89,* 170–182.

Graham, S., & Harris, K. R. (2000). The role of self-regulation and transcription skills in writing and writing development. *Educational Psychologist, 35,* 3–12.

Hayes, J. R. (1996). A new framework for understanding cognition and affect in writing. In C. M. Levy & S. Ransdell (Eds.), *The science of writing: Theories, methods, individual differences, and applications* (pp. 1–27). Mahwah, NJ: Lawrence Erlbaum Associates, Inc.

Hayes, J. R., & Flower, L. S. (1980). Identifying the organization of writing processes. In L. W. Gregg & E. R. Steinberg (Eds.), *Cognitive processes in writing* (pp. 3–30). Hillsdale, NJ: Lawrence Erlbaum Associates, Inc.

Hidi, S., & Hildyard, A. (1983). The comparison of oral and written productions of two discourse types. *Discourse Processes, 6,* 91–105.

Just, M. A., & Carpenter, P. A. (1992). A capacity theory of comprehension: Individual differences in working memory. *Psychological Review, 99,* 122–149.

Kellogg, R. T. (1987). Effects of topic knowledge on the allocation of processing time and cognitive effort to writing processes. *Memory & Cognition, 15,* 256–266.

Kellogg, R. T. (1996). A model of working memory in writing. In C. M. Levy & S. Ransdell (Eds.), *The science of writing: Theories, methods, individual differences, and applications* (pp. 57–71). Mahwah, NJ: Lawrence Erlbaum Associates, Inc.

King, M., & Rentel, V. (1981). Research update: Conveying meaning in written texts. *Language Arts, 58,* 721–728.

Kintsch, W. (1998). *Comprehension: A paradigm for cognition.* New York: Cambridge University Press.

Kintsch, W., & van Dijk, T. A. (1978). Toward a model of text comprehension and production. *Psychological Review, 85,* 363–394.

Langer, J. A. (1984). The effects of available information on responses to school writing tasks. *Research in the Teaching of English, 18,* 27–44.

Langer, J. A. (1986). *Children reading and writing: Structures and strategies.* Norwood, NJ: Ablex.

Langer, J. A. (1992). Speaking and knowing: Conceptions of understanding in academic disciplines. In A. Herrington & C. Moran (Eds.), *Writing, teaching, and learning in the disciplines* (pp. 68–85). New York: Modern Language Association.

Levy, C. M., & Ransdell, S. (1995). Is writing as difficult as it seems? *Memory & Cognition, 23,* 767–779.

Littleton, E. B. (1998). Emerging cognitive skills for writing: Sensitivity to audience presence in five- through nine-year olds' speech. *Cognition and Instruction, 16,* 399–430.

MacDonald, S. P. (1992). A method for analyzing sentence-level differences in disciplinary knowledge making. *Written Communication, 9,* 533–569.

Matsuhashi, A. (1982). Explorations in the real-time production of written discourse. In M. Nystrand (Ed.), *What writers know: The language, process, and structure of written texts* (pp. 269–290). New York: Academic.

McCutchen, D. (1984). Writing as a linguistic problem. *Educational Psychologist, 19,* 226–238.

McCutchen, D. (1986). Domain knowledge and linguistic knowledge in the development of writing ability. *Journal of Memory and Language, 25,* 431–444.

McCutchen, D. (1987). Children's discourse skill: Form and modality requirements of schooled writing. *Discourse Processes, 10,* 267–286.

McCutchen, D. (1988). "Functional automaticity" in children's writing: A problem of metacognitive control. *Written Communication, 5,* 306–324.

McCutchen, D. (1994). The magical number three, plus or minus two: Working memory in writing. In J. S. Carlson (Series Ed.) & E. C. Butterfield (Vol. Ed.), *Advances in cognition and educational practice, Vol. 2. Children's writing. Toward a process theory of the development of skilled writing.* Greenwich, CT: JAI.

McCutchen, D. (1996). A capacity theory of writing: Working memory in composition. *Educational Psychology Review, 8,* 299–325.

McCutchen, D., Abbott, R. D., Green, L. B., Beretvas, S. N., Cox, S., Potter, N. S., Quiroga, T., & Gray, A. L. (in press). Beginning literacy: Links among teacher knowledge, teacher practice, and student learning. *Journal of Learning Disabilities.*

McCutchen, D., Covill, A., Hoyne, S. H., & Mildes, K. (1994). Individual differences in writing: Implications of translating fluency. *Journal of Educational Psychology, 86,* 256–266.

McCutchen, D., Francis, M., & Kerr, S. (1997). Revising for meaning: Effects of knowledge and strategy. *Journal of Educational Psychology, 89,* 667–676.

McCutchen, D., & Perfetti, C. A. (1982). Coherence and connectedness in the development of discourse production. *Text, 2,* 113–139.

McNamara, D. S., & Kintsch, W. (1996). Working memory in text comprehension: Interrupting difficult text. In *The Seventeenth Proceedings of the Cognitive Science Society.* Mahwah, NJ: Lawrence Erlbaum Associates, Inc.

Means, M. L., & Voss, J. F. (1985). Star wars: A developmental study of expert and novice knowledge structures. *Journal of Memory and Language, 24,* 746–757.

Miller, G. A. (1956). The magical number seven, plus or minus two: Some limits on our capacity for processing information. *Psychological Review, 63,* 81–97.

Miyake, A., Just, M. A., & Carpenter, P. A. (1994). Working memory constraints on the resolution of lexical ambiguity: Maintaining multiple interpretations in neutral contexts. *Journal of Memory and Language, 33,* 175–202.

Montague, M., Graves, A., & Leavell, A. (1991). Planning, procedural facilitation, and narrative composition of junior high students with learning disabilities. *Learning Disabilities Research & Practice, 6,* 219–224.

Myers, G. (1985). Text as knowledge claims: The social construction of two biologists' proposals. *Written Communication, 2,* 219–245.

Peskin, J. (1998). Constructing meaning when reading poetry: An expert–novice study. *Cognition and Instruction, 16*, 235–263.

Ransdell, S., & Levy, C. M. (1996). Working memory constraints on writing quality and fluency. In C. M. Levy & S. Ransdell (Eds.), *The science of writing: Theories, methods, individual differences, and applications* (pp. 93–105). Mahwah, NJ: Lawrence Erlbaum Associates, Inc.

Spilich, G. J., Vesonder, G. T., Chiesi, H. L., & Voss, J. F. (1979). Text processing of domain related information for individuals with high and low domain knowledge. *Journal of Verbal Learning and Verbal Behavior, 18*, 275–290.

Stein, N. L., & Glenn, C. G. (1979). An analysis of story comprehension in elementary school children. In R. O. Freedle (Ed.), *Advances in discourse processing: Vol. 2. New directions in discourse processing* (pp. 53–120). Norwood, NJ: Ablex.

Stockton, S. (1995). Writing in history: Narrating the subject of time. *Written Communication, 12*, 47–73.

Sulzby, E. (1985). Kindergartners as writers and readers. In M. Farr (Ed.), *Advances in writing research: Vol. 1. Children's early writing development* (pp. 127–199). Norwood, NJ: Ablex.

Sulzby, E., & Teale, W. (1987). *Young children's storybook reading: Longitudinal study of parent child interactions and children's independent functioning.* Final report to Spencer Foundation. Ann Arbor: University of Michigan Press.

Swanson, H. L. (1992). The generality and modifiability of working memory. *Journal of Educational Psychology, 84*, 473–488.

Tetroe, J. (1984, April). *Information processing demand of plot construction in story writing.* Paper presented at the meeting of the American Educational Research Association, New Orleans.

Vande Kopple, W. J. (1998). Relative clauses in spectroscopic articles in the *Physical Review*, Beginnings and 1980: Some changes in patterns of modification and a connection to possible shifts in style. *Written Communication, 15*, 170–202.

Voss, J. F., Vesonder, G. T., & Spilich, G. J. (1980). Text generation and recall by high-knowledge and low-knowledge individuals. *Journal of Verbal Learning and Verbal Behavior, 19*, 651–667.

Wineburg, S. S. (1991). On the reading of historical texts: Notes on the breach between school and the academy. *American Educational Research Journal, 28*, 495–519.

EDUCATIONAL PSYCHOLOGIST, 35(1), 25–37

Developing Motivation to Write

Roger Bruning and Christy Horn

Center for Instructional Innovation
University of Nebraska–Lincoln

Two decades of cognitive research have shown writing to be a highly fluid process of problem solving requiring constant monitoring of progress toward task goals. Becoming an able writer brings great intellectual and social rewards, but the extended nature and difficulty of this process create unique motivational challenges. Speech development provides some models for development of writing motivation, but writing requires special attention to motivational conditions. Four clusters of conditions are proposed as keys to developing motivation: nurturing functional beliefs about writing, fostering engagement using authentic writing tasks, providing a supportive context for writing, and creating a positive emotional environment. Teachers' own conceptions of writing are seen as crucial to establishing these conditions in most writing contexts. Systematic motivational research complementing our knowledge about the cognitive processes of writing is needed to understand the development of motivation to write.

Random scribbles on paper or a handy wall signal the beginning of a lifetime of writing for most children. From these humble beginnings, writing's course moves ahead predictably, although certainly not at the same pace for every child. Scribbles soon become more letter-like, giving way to true letters and words. As writing development proceeds in the school years, we see increases in young writers' range of lexical choices, sentence complexity, and topical coherence. They begin to shift away from list-like writing and localized control (e.g., linking to vocabulary used in the previous sentence, repeating familiar syntactic frames) toward a more goal-directed, strategic approach (Berninger, Fuller, & Whitaker, 1996). Their writing has more topical and thematic coherence (e.g., Flower et al., 1990), as purpose, planning, and revising play an increasing role. A growing metacognitive capability gives them the potential to shift from a knowledge-telling to a knowledge-transforming approach (Bereiter & Scardamalia, 1987) and to use information about audience, genre, and rhetorical stance to accomplish a variety of writing purposes (Berninger et al., 1996).

Ideally, these developmental processes result in highly capable and motivated writers, able to deploy a variety of approaches as their purposes and audiences change. They see writing as entering a kind of conversation (Boice, 1994) leading to self-understanding and interaction with others. They hold positive views not only about writing's utility, but about engaging in its processes, and approach writing with anticipation, feelings of control, and minimal anxiety. Their writing production is steady and relatively stress free; they somehow have struck balances between impatience and procrastination, between dull habit and anxious waiting for inspiration.

For many of us, unfortunately, this idealized portrait of writing development may not be a particularly accurate depiction of our own writing development. More important for our purposes here, our collective shortcomings in developing our students' ability and motivation to write are all too apparent. The latest National Center for Education Statistics (1997) writing assessment, for example, shows that although more than 80% of eleventh graders in the United States can begin to write focused and clear responses to tasks, fewer than one third can write complete responses containing sufficient information to support their claims. Only 2% can write effective responses containing supporting details and discussion.

On the attitudinal side, evidence of our failing to develop positive beliefs and motivation toward writing abounds. There is, of course, the lore of great writing—that if it isn't spontaneously inspired it must be heroically painful. Writing is easy, said Gene Fowler in a famous quip, you " … simply sit staring at a blank sheet of paper until the drops of blood form on your forehead." From the vantage point of his clinical practice in helping people who want and need to write, Boice (1994) observed that his clients, typically individuals who have experienced a fair amount of writing success, too often

---

Requests for reprints should be sent to Roger Bruning, Center for Instructional Innovation, University of Nebraska–Lincoln, 212 Bancroft Hall, Lincoln, NE 68588-0384. E-mail: rbruning@unl.edu

"force writing with a hurried pace, a lagging confidence, and a lingering malaise," remaining ambivalent about writing and "inconsistent about turning intentions into actions" (p. 1). These feelings are no strangers to the masses of our students; although they believe that writing is important and are quite certain of its link to success in school and life (e.g., Shell, Colvin, & Bruning, 1995), the thought of writing, especially extended writing, evokes in them what could best be described as a mixed reaction. For too many, the motivational balance tilts negatively—toward feelings of anxiety and dread, lack of control, and avoidance (Cleary, 1991).

Although it seems that we have much to learn about developing motivation to write, we do have a solid understanding about the processes of writing itself, much of it acquired in the past 2 decades. Research both in the cognitive sciences (e.g., Bereiter & Scardamalia, 1987; Flower & Hayes, 1981; Flower et al., 1990; Flower, Wallace, Norris, & Burnett, 1994; Levy & Ransdell, 1996) and in the literary tradition (e.g., Applebee & Langer, 1984; Elbow, 1994; Langer, 1992; Spaulding, 1992) has provided a converging picture of writing as a process of meaning making and has shifted emphasis away from writing mechanics to an emphasis on communication. We now recognize skilled writing for what it is—a tremendously complex problem-solving act involving memory, planning, text generation, and revision (Flower et al., 1990, 1994). In solving writing's ill-defined problems, writers must juggle multiple goals (Hayes, 1996) and satisfy many constraints—of topic, audience, purpose, and of physically creating the text itself. They also must switch back and forth among a variety of frames of reference, including critical thinking (e.g., perspective, logic), rhetorical stances (e.g., description, persuasion), and writing conventions (e.g., tone, mechanics, spelling). In a difficult and complex task like this, motivational issues will assume particularly prominent status. Writers need to develop strong beliefs in the relevance and importance of writing and, as they grapple with writing's complexities and frustrations, learn to be patient, persistent, and flexible. Although we believe that these beliefs and attitudes ultimately fall clearly within the realm of intrinsic motivation, their development is in the hands of those who set the writing tasks and react to what has been written.

THE NEED TO EMPHASIZE MOTIVATION TO WRITE

This article focuses on conditions affecting the development of motivation to write. As rich as cognitive research has been in helping us understand writing, it has only scratched the surface of the issue of motivational and social-cognitive variables (e.g., see Bergin & LaFave, 1998; Hayes, 1996; Spaulding, 1992). We argue, therefore, for an expansion of our models to more explicitly recognize the social-cognitive variables implicit in these cognitive analyses. Literacy researchers have long recognized this

need—of not only helping students learn how to write, but learn how to want to write (Spaulding, 1992). A vast number of books and articles, many in the whole-language tradition (e.g., Calkins, 1994; Graves, 1991, 1994), have addressed issues of student interest, engagement, and motivation. As Spaulding pointed out, however, most of these have remained largely unconnected to the rapidly growing research in motivation. Although there is a wealth of practical knowledge about writing instruction, there is still relatively little in the way of scientific analysis aimed at the motivational factors critical to writing development.

In this article, we examine issues affecting development of motivation to write and provide a general framework for research aimed at understanding its development. We make several assumptions. The first is that the root source of motivation to write is a set of beliefs about writing, many of them tacit. As Flower et al. (1990) pointed out, writers' conceptions of the writing task—tacit or not—inevitably affect what they write. Their task representations guide a set of critical decisions, setting up strategies for completing the tasks and creating bridges between writing processes and products. Motivational considerations are an integral part of their vision as writers make trade-offs between costs and benefits of various goals and ways to use resources (Flower et al., 1994; Hayes, 1996). In any writing task—from a child's brief book report to the reading-to-write assignment of college composition—writers must negotiate between what is expected and what can be done. Students need to be motivated to enter, persist, and succeed in this ill-defined problem space we call writing.

A second assumption is that the wellspring of motivation is experiencing writing as purposeful, authentic communication (Crystal, 1997). Like speakers, writers must express themselves in writing, seeing it not so much as a product but as a way of entering and participating in a discourse community (Boice, 1994). In such communities, the central guiding and nurturing force is the teacher whose conceptions of writing will provide a model for and shape students' beliefs. Thus, we argue, programs for developing writing motivation will rest on the beliefs that teachers themselves hold.

A third assumption is that understanding motivation to write requires an appreciation of writing's relation to oral language. A comparison is useful if for no other reason than the phenomenal success children have learning to speak. By the age of four, virtually every child has learned to speak and has done so in the absence of any formal instruction. Many of the conditions supporting this remarkable developmental achievement can be enlisted to support children's writing. However, understanding how writing development differs from speech development is also critical. We believe the comparability argument is overextended by those who argue that simply creating a literacy-rich environment is sufficient. Learning to write is an extraordinarily complex linguistic and cognitive task requiring close attention to the conditions for developing motivation and skill. Because it is typically further removed from experience, writing often lacks the accompanying web of context that supports oral discourse. The challenge for the writer is to recreate the experience—in other words, recontextualize it—without the immediacy of oral discourse (C. A. Cameron, Hunt, & Linton, 1996). Snow (1983) argued that learning to read is facilitated by oral language experiences where parents scaffold understanding by speaking in literate ways. Writing needs the same kind of structure. Because written discourse contains many unfamiliar elements (e.g., new discourse forms, conventions of writing) and exposes writers' thoughts and feelings to much closer scrutiny, careful planning is required to develop positive motivation for the act and process of writing.

Table 1 contrasts the oral language capabilities most children bring to school and the challenges that writing presents. Our portrayal, which draws on Calfee's views (e.g., see Calfee & Patrick, 1995), emphasizes the natural language dimensions of children's early oral language experience, contrasting them with the features of language that children encounter through becoming literate. By its very nature, writing typically is a more deliberate, formal act than speech, one that reveals the linguistic and cognitive processes supporting it (Olson, 1994).

Although posing considerable motivational challenges, writing's formal qualities are what give it its potential for developing students' abilities to understand, organize, and express their thoughts and feelings. Developing writers are challenged to do far more than simply set down a sequence of words. They must learn a new communication framework involving an intricate set of formal language conventions. They must spell out what topics are about, organize information, and provide causal explanations. The feedback students receive soon uncovers another feature of written language—its ability to show the quality and authenticity of a writer's thoughts and feelings. When language is written down, anybody can see whether ideas are logical and fit together, or whether emotions ring true. Students doing an investigative

report on, for instance, the safety of school playground equipment not only need to state important facts, but express them well and persuasively. Student writing seldom rises to be as vivid and engaging as the stories and word pictures of conversation, but it serves vital developmental purposes by placing new demands on the student. The motivational challenge is to help students see that writing's benefits outweigh its considerable effort and risks.

DEVELOPING MOTIVATION TO WRITE

We now turn to the factors we believe are most important for developing and maintaining motivation to write. In describing them, we draw on our analysis of the nature of written discourse, on the relatively small current research literature directly linking motivational constructs and writing, and, as appropriate, on the much larger literatures relating to motivation in general and to writing instructional practices. Table 2 provides the four clusters of conditions we consider most critical in developing writing motivation, together with exemplars of interventions likely to affect writing motivation's development. These clusters also provide a framework for research leading to a comprehensive understanding of how writing motivation develops.

Heading the list of motivation-enhancing conditions, in our judgment, is *nurturing functional beliefs about the nature of writing and its outcomes*. These beliefs have multiple dimensions, starting with a realistic appraisal of the difficulties and challenges of writing. They also include beliefs in writing's potential, in one's capabilities as a writer, and in having control over writing tasks. A second cluster is designed *to foster student engagement through authentic goals and contexts*—in other words, writing that students will see as meaningful, purposeful, and allowing them to express their own voice (Elbow, 1994; Oldfather, 1993; Oldfather & Dahl, 1994). The goal is to find tasks that generate engagement through their intrinsic qualities and require a minimum of ex-

TABLE 1
Typical Features of Children's Experience With Oral and Written Discourse

Oral Discourse	Written Discourse
Rapid, transitory, inexact, variable. Provision of additional information is major mechanism for refining meanings and correcting errors.	Slow developing, stable, and reproduceable. Revision in light of communication purpose and audience is critical for clarifying ideas and communicating effectively.
Contextual and implicit. Listeners can "fill in" meaning using a variety of contextual clues.	Decontextualized and explicit. Writers must establish common ground for understanding, considering factors such as purpose, audience, and writing conventions.
Early, high, continuing exposure. Most children immersed in rich discourse communities that link oral language to all parts of their lives.	Later, lower, more intermittent exposure. Most children entering school are relative novices at writing, unsure about writing's uses and their own capabilities.
Highly varied pragmatic uses. Most beginning students skilled at using natural language to describe things, tell stories, and express their feelings.	Narrower range of uses. Most entering students will not yet have used writing pragmatically and need to discover writing's utility for description, self-expression, and persuasion.
Narrative structures dominate. Communication success depends on imagery, memorability, implicit meanings.	Descriptive, logical structures dominate. Writing permits careful examination of cognitive and emotional dimensions of communication. Successful writing requires mastery of formal language conventions.

TABLE 2
Factors in Developing Motivation to Write

Cluster	Related Motivation-Enhancing Conditions
Nurturing functional beliefs about writing	• Creating a classroom community supporting writing and other literacy activities • Displaying the ways that teachers use writing personally • Finding writing tasks that assure student success • Providing opportunities for students to build expertise in areas they will write about • Using brief daily writing activities to encourage regular writing • Encouraging writing in a wide variety of genres
Fostering student engagement through authentic writing goals and contexts	• Having students find examples of different kinds of writing (e.g., self-expressive, persuasive, entertaining) • Encouraging students to write about topics of personal interest • Having students write for a variety of audiences • Establishing improved communication as purpose for revision • Integrating writing into instruction in other disciplines (e.g., science, math, social studies)
Providing a supportive context for writing	• Breaking complex writing tasks into parts • Encouraging goal setting and monitoring of progress • Assisting students in setting writing goals that are neither too challenging nor too simple • Teaching writing strategies and helping students learn to monitor their use • Giving feedback on progress toward writing goals • Using peers as writing partners in literacy communities
Creating a positive emotional environment	• Modeling positive attitudes toward writing • Creating a safe environment for writing • Giving students choices about what they will write • Providing feedback allowing students to retain control over their writing • Utilizing natural outcomes (e.g., communication success) as feedback source • Training students to engage in positive self-talk about writing • Helping students reframe anxiety, stress as natural arousal

ternally managed rewards to keep students involved. A third group of conditions involves *providing a supportive context to develop requisite writing skills*. They include task framing, practice, and feedback conditions likely to build skills and motivation. The final cluster of conditions focuses on *creating a positive emotional environment*, where ideas and feelings can be expressed safely. Because even the most ideal course of writing development involves challenge and frustration, students' anxieties and frustrations with writing also must be addressed. For each of these clusters, we outline possibilities for research on writing motivation.

Cluster 1: Nurturing Functional Beliefs About Writing

Except when carried out mechanically or under duress, writing is a volitional act of problem solving (e.g., Flower et al., 1990; Hayes, 1996). Success in almost any writing task requires extended periods of concentration and engagement in which writers must marshal all of their cognitive, motivational, and linguistic resources. Beliefs about writing must be sufficiently potent to carry the writer through the difficult and often emotion-laden processes of writing.

A reasonable starting point is the perception that writing has value (Codling & Gambrell, 1997). Most students, in fact, seem to believe that it does, at least for achieving academic and vocational goals. Shell et al. (1995) and Pajares and his associates (Pajares & Johnson, 1996; Pajares, Miller, & Johnson, 1999; Pajares & Valiante, 1997), for instance, showed that perceived usefulness of writing is already high by the upper-elementary grades, with writing continuing to be highly valued into high school and college (Shell, Murphy, & Bruning, 1989).

Belief in one's competence as a writer also seems essential to writing motivation. Because of its consistent relation to writing performance (Pajares & Johnson, 1996; Pajares et al., 1999; Pajares & Valiante, 1997; Shell et al., 1989, 1995) and solid theoretical grounding (Bandura, 1997; Schunk, 1991), self-efficacy has emerged as a major focus in studies of writing motivation. Extending self-efficacy theory to writing leads to predictions of a reciprocal relation between writing skill and efficacy, with such assumed benefits for high efficacy writers as lower anxiety, greater persistence, and higher toleration for frustration in writing tasks.

Writing self-efficacy appears to follow a developmental course, most likely linked to growth in writing competence; compared to fourth graders, both seventh and tenth graders have higher self-efficacy for completing writing tasks (Shell et al., 1995). Writing efficacy also increases as a result of interventions that provide students with tools for improving their writing skills. Graham and Harris (1989a, 1989b) and Schunk and Swartz (1993) showed, for example, that the development of self-efficacy for writing is linked to whether students have strategies for writing and to the kinds of feedback they receive. In Graham and Harris's work, students who were learning disabled who were taught strategies for writing stories and essays increased both their writing skills and self-efficacy, changes that were maintained and transferred to other settings. In studies with upper elementary students, Schunk and Swartz highlighted *process goals,* involving strategies that upper-elementary students could use to improve their writing, and *progress feedback,* where experimenters provided students with information on how well they were learning to use a writing strategy. Process goals appear to have some independent effects, and combining process goals with progress feedback not only brings about improvements in self-efficacy, but also increases both strategy use and writing skill. Schunk and Swartz argued that, in general, progress feedback raises efficacy by conveying a belief to learners that they are capable of continuing to improve their skills. It may also heighten learners' sense of volitional control over their writing (Corno, 1993; Deci, Vallerand, Pelletier, & Ryan, 1991; Turner, 1995).

Gender also appears to play a role in the development of writing efficacy. Pajares and Valiente (1997) found, for example, that fifth-grade boys and girls did not differ in their writing performance but that girls perceived writing as more useful than boys, had greater self-efficacy, and worried less about it. In a sample of ninth graders, however, girls reported lower self-efficacy than boys, even though their actual writing performance did not differ. These findings may reflect a general downward trend for girls in perceptions of their academic competence (Phillips & Zimmerman, 1990). It may also be, as Cleary (1996) argued, that secondary schools and colleges emphasize a male-biased form of discourse requiring females to adapt to structures that may be less intuitive, interesting, or intrinsically motivating.

Writers, no doubt, hold a range of important motivation-relevant beliefs that extend well beyond ideas of its value and their own writing competence. Some of these likely parallel the implicit beliefs shown to have important motivational consequences in other areas (e.g., Dweck & Leggett, 1988; Schraw & Bruning, 1996, 1999). Dweck and Leggett, for example, demonstrated that individuals holding so-called incremental views about intelligence (i.e., that intelligence is changeable) tend to have a learning or mastery orientation and, when faced with challenging conditions, respond with more persistent and flexible problem solving. Complex literacy tasks have been found to promote mastery responses because they challenge students (Miller, Adkins, & Hooper, 1993). Environments that provide students the opportunity for input and choice, promote student interaction, and provide challenging tasks particularly impact the goal orientations of lower ability students in positive ways (Meece & Miller, 1999). Similarly, Schraw, Bruning, and their associates (Bruning, Horn, & Sodoro, 1998; Schraw & Bruning, 1996) showed that individuals' implicit beliefs that reading is

transactional lead to higher levels of reading engagement and affects reading choices.

Directions for future research.   Although there has been substantial research on writing self-efficacy, plus some work on attributions for writing success (e.g., Shell et al., 1995) and writing apprehension (e.g., Madigan, Linton, & Johnson, 1996), less is known about the patterns of other beliefs that students hold about writing and how they develop. Is there, for example, a parallel to the belief structures identified by Dweck and Leggett (1988), where some students take an entity view of writing, assuming that their writing ability is largely fixed? If so, are there negative motivational consequences, such as those that accompany a performative outlook (e.g., excessive concern with evaluation, risk aversion)? The work of Palmquist and Young (1992) hinted at this possibility; students who believe strongly that writing is a gift (i.e., an entity view) show significantly more writing anxiety and assess their own capabilities more negatively. Similarly, comparable to Schraw and Bruning's (1996, 1999) findings on the structure of reading beliefs, do some see writing as an act of information transmission, whereas others see it as much more transactional? If patterns of writing beliefs vary along this dimension, how do they relate to the likelihood of adopting, for example, a knowledge-telling versus a knowledge-transforming approach in writing (Bereiter & Scardamalia, 1987)? Also, how may such beliefs relate to willingness to revise and to choices about the kinds of revisions to make (Graham, 1997), two critical factors in shaping writers' development?

Several additional dimensions potentially important for developing writing motivation also remain largely unexplored. One of these is beliefs about writing's social role. In many classrooms, writing is structured as a dispassionate and possibly gender-biased activity where only the "academic voice" is valued (Cleary, 1996; McCracken, 1992). Likewise, idea generation, information gathering, writing, and revising can be solitary and potentially isolating acts. Contrasting to these conditions is writing in literacy-oriented classrooms where writing and talk about writing are central features of the classrooms' intellectual and social life and where a variety of expressive forms are honored. Features of such classrooms are well-known (Bruning & Schweiger, 1997; Calfee & Patrick, 1995; Guthrie & Alao, 1997; Guthrie & McCann, 1997; Graves, 1991; Turner, 1995); they include making literacy activities the classroom centerpiece, encouraging cooperative activities, creating project-oriented tasks, giving students responsibility, and scaffolding student responses to insure success. The centrality of literacy and writing in particular seem likely to widen students' understanding of the social functions of written language and to help fulfill a host of social and relational needs. Key questions for the development of motivation to write are whether these experiences affect students' beliefs about writing and, if so, which of the conditions are most critical.

Cluster 2: Fostering Student Engagement Through Authentic Writing Goals and Contexts

Schools provide the best and often the only real opportunities most children have to write. Beyond the simple opportunity to write, of course, is the quality of the writing experience, which is largely determined by how teachers use writing in their classes. Their actions and the enthusiasm they portray toward writing provide the models for student perceptions of writing. Teachers play a vital role by choosing appropriately challenging literacy assignments that foster student engagement and motivation (Ames & Archer, 1988, Guthrie & Alao, 1997; Guthrie & McCann, 1997; Lepper & Hodell, 1989). Another critical role comes in providing guidance and ongoing feedback on writing.

For elementary-level students, in particular, teacher guidance and feedback has a significant impact on the development of strategies, confidence, and actual writing performance (Pajares & Johnson, 1996; Skinner, Wellborn, & Connell, 1990). Teachers can help break writing tasks into manageable parts, which not only reduces the processing demands of a complex task, but also allows students to monitor their progress and experience success during the writing process. Embedded in the tasks teachers assign is the information that shapes students' beliefs about their ability, the amount of effort they are willing to expend, and satisfaction (Ames, 1992). Cycles of goal setting coupled with feedback regarding progress toward the goals often are necessary to activate a full capability for self-monitoring and self-regulation (Cervone, 1993).

Whether teachers enact these important steps depends greatly on what they believe about writing. Their decisions about writing's place in the curriculum—and their reactions to student writing—trace back to their own understanding of writings' nature, its uses, and their own feelings toward it. Thus, the beginning point for building student writing motivation is teacher beliefs about writing. If teachers' experiences with writing are narrow-gauge, socially isolating, evaluation oriented, and anxiety provoking, they are very unlikely to be able to create positive motivational conditions for their students' writing. On the other hand, if teachers see writing as a critical tool for intellectual and social development and as serving a broad range of important student aims—for cognitive stimulation and growth, self-expression, or social affiliation—they will provide settings aimed at fostering similar beliefs.

School writing often takes place under conditions that are artificial, at least from the students' perspective. Writing tasks such as abstracting chapters and books, completing essay exams, and writing term papers seem largely of the teacher's making. Even when selected for sound pedagogical reasons, writing activities often are not set within larger social or communication frames that can create interest and a sense of writing's relevance. Writing becomes an "assignment" in

which the desire for closure around specific conclusions will be very strong (Flower et al., 1990). Absent from such arrangements is the opportunity to see writing's utility for "real" purposes such as persuasion, description, and expressing the writer's voice. What is needed, in the view of many, are authentic literacy tasks (e.g., Cleary, 1991; Turner, 1995).

Hiebert (1994) described authentic literacy tasks as activities that involve children in the immediate use of literacy for enjoyment and communication, distinguishing them from activities where literacy skills are acquired for some unspecified future use. Traditionally, pursuing activities within real-world social and physical contexts has been strongly emphasized (e.g., Brown, Collins, & Duguid, 1989). Many also would add the criterion of meaningfulness, of students acquiring skills within rather than separate from the contexts in which they will be used. Ideally, authentic tasks have much in common with the best of real-world experience—affording opportunities for challenge and self-improvement, student autonomy, interest-based learning, and social interaction (Turner, 1995).

Having genuine reasons for writing almost certainly has motivational consequences. Authentic tasks would seem to afford students the opportunity to express and refine their voice (e.g., Elbow, 1994; Schiwy, 1996). Words set down on a page to a real audience for a real purpose are their own, not borrowed (Elbow, 1994). Authentic tasks are likely to help students develop one or more distinctive styles of writing and to determine if these styles are "theirs." They may also develop more complex dimensions of voice, such as learning to write with authority or ironically. Such writing has potential for expressing "the person behind the words" (Elbow, 1994) and for revealing dimensions of the writer's identity, character, and goals. Writers' discoveries of their own voice and their growing ability to express it would seem to have considerable potential for developing motivation to write (Oldfather, 1993; Oldfather & Dahl, 1994).

Interest is another powerful motivator. It has been shown to have two primary functions: determining how long students persist at tasks and the level of attention they are willing to commit (Hidi, 1990) and influencing the goals students set for themselves, particularly if they see writing as a mechanism by which they can meet their communication needs (Csikszentmihalyi & Rathunde, 1993). The research on the impact of interest on writing has revealed a complex relation between knowledge, interest, and writing performance (Benton, Corkill, Sharp, Downey, & Khramtsova, 1995; Hidi & Anderson, 1992). Benton et al. (1995), for example, found that students with high topic knowledge and high interest wrote essays that included content-relevant information that was logical and well-organized, whereas writers with relatively less interest and knowledge generated more ideas unrelated to the topic. Although there was a strong relation between knowledge and interest, they were found to be separate constructs. Studies with middle-school children conducted by Pintrich and DeGroot (1990) showed that students who believed that they were engaged in important and interesting tasks were more cognitively strategic.

Directions for future research. Although a host of theoretical and practical considerations strongly recommend use of authentic tasks and contexts for writing, there is as yet little empirical support for their use or even understanding of their nature. In general, we know that tasks involving variety and diversity are more likely to create interest in learning and a mastery orientation (Ames, 1992). In writing, however, we do not have any kind of taxonomy relating different kinds of writing tasks to either skill or motivational development. What effects do response journals or personal essays, for example, have on the quality of students' creative self-expression and on their desire to write?

More generally, what are the motivational effects exerted by the set of conditions that we refer to as *authentic writing contexts?* It may be useful to approach this question by systematically inquiring into those features of writing contexts, goals, and feedback conditions that most affect motivation to write. For instance, what are the motivational effects if there are pragmatic purposes for writing beyond completion of the assignment itself, or when writing tasks are embedded in larger task contexts? How is writing affected when the audience shifts to one the writer sees as important—to younger students or pen pals in a partner school, for example, or to parents, business people, or public officials?

We also need to inquire of students themselves—about those purposes of writing they consider to be most meaningful and motivating. Are their conceptions consonant with ours? Of all the features of context and purpose, which contribute systematically to student perceptions that writing is interesting and meaningful? How can these features be operationalized for writers of different ages and abilities? Finally, is it always necessary or even desirable to set writing within "real-world" social and physical environments, or are factors such as the opportunity for challenge, student autonomy, interest, and social interaction (Turner, 1995) more reliable keys to student motivation to write?

Cluster 3: Providing a Supportive Context for Writing

Writing successfully is a complex and effortful activity requiring systematic attention to motivational conditions. Each act of writing takes place in a context that defines the initial nature of the writing task, affects the goals that writers set, and influences the decisions they will make as writing progresses (Hayes, 1996). Context also determines the level of skill required to complete a writing task successfully. For students to engage fully and succeed in writing, they need to be able to tap motivational resources embedded in the task itself (e.g., its perceived utility), in their own interests and motivational histories, and in the feedback they receive or give themselves during the writing process.

Gaining and maintaining control of a writing task almost certainly are critical motivationally. No matter what the writer's developmental stage or ability level, each act of writing poses a formidable challenge, having much in common with other ill-defined problems (Flower et al., 1990). In creating the problem space and in its later refinements, writers must balance the potential costs of various courses of action with their hypothesized benefits (Hayes, 1996). Do I need more information? Do I need to change the focus of what I'm writing? Do I have time to revise? Should I read over the paper one more time? Parameters defining this fluctuating problem space include the writer's purposes for writing, the norms of the discourse community (as embodied by the teacher or other audiences), and the writer's own knowledge and writing skill. Framed too broadly, this ill-defined problem has the potential of overwhelming the writer—unless the writer has clear goals and can deploy strategies to reach them. If a writer embarks on a writing journey with a too-complex problem definition, the results can be disastrous, especially if approaches are abandoned midstream (Cervone, 1993).

Given a choice between complexity and simplicity, however, it seems better to err in the direction of complexity in selecting writing tasks. Students find cognitively complex learning activities inherently more interesting and demanding of mental effort (Meece & Miller, 1992); such tasks lead to higher levels of motivation because they create interest, allow for self-improvement, and afford opportunities to control one's own learning (Turner, 1995). They prefer complex literacy assignments for much the same reasons (Miller et al., 1993). Writers need to believe, however, that if the task is complex it can be accomplished with reasonable effort. This belief can be fostered by helping students define tasks in terms of proximal goals with clear definitions of what constitutes success, learn to observe and judge their own performance against these goals, and react appropriately to these judgments (e.g., by working harder or changing strategies; Schunk & Zimmerman, 1994). In addition, students' engagement levels increase when they consider tasks to be meaningful and connect their accomplishments to their effort (Lepper & Hodell, 1989; Meece, 1991; Nicholls, 1984; Wigfield, Eccles, & Rodriguez, 1998).

Although complex writing tasks can be desirable, students' responses to them need careful monitoring. When they perceive tasks as too difficult or ambiguous, cooperation and interest may decrease and they may try to negotiate requirements downward (Doyle, 1986). Needlessly complex assignments or immature writers' own poor judgments also can place them in situations too complex for them to handle and push them, as Larson (1995) stated, outside their "performance envelopes." When writing tasks take students beyond their ability, the result likely will be anxiety that will lead to poorly controlled writing. If anxiety rises to a high level, the result may be emotional and cognitive thrashing that disrupts writing entirely. Again, at the other end of the spectrum, the result if expectations are too low will be low motivation characterized by apathy, boredom, or disinterest.

Helping students set specific challenging goals.   Successful writing depends on students' ability to manage an ongoing relation between themselves and their writing, establishing a level of engagement that maintains their attention and keeps them motivated and involved (Larson, 1995). The challenges are to engage developing writers in writing tasks that match their abilities and current motivational levels and to help them develop the habits and strategies that keep them moving ahead productively (e.g., Graham, 1997). A large amount of motivational literature points to goal setting and progress monitoring as two consistently facilitative variables in this regard. Goals, especially if they are specific and challenging, will lead to higher levels of performance. They will have their greatest effect, however, when students have accurate and useful feedback during task engagement (Locke & Latham, 1990).

Writers necessarily alter their goals as they compose; a key to maintaining motivation to write lies in how these alterations take place. For novice writers and even for quite skilled ones, abandoning one set of goals and starting toward others can create a situation from which it is difficult to recover. Writers instead need to maintain a balance between the challenges presented by the task at any given point and their skills, interest level, and confidence to successfully complete the task (Larson, 1995).

Work by Graham, Harris, and their colleagues (e.g., Graham, 1997; Graham & Harris, 1989a; Graham, MacArthur, & Schwartz, 1995) and by Schunk and his associates (Schunk & Rice, 1991; Schunk & Swartz, 1993) points toward the utility of a combination of goal setting, goal-related strategies, and process feedback. Specific goals for writing, coupled with strategy instruction, facilitate both writing quality and efficacy (e.g., Graham, 1997; Graham et al., 1995). The addition of procedural support for strategies (Graham, 1997) and feedback on how students are progressing toward acquiring writing strategies provides information that the strategies being employed are useful and the students are increasing their skills (Borkowski, Weyhing, & Carr, 1988; Graham & Harris, 1993). These factors are particularly critical in improving self-efficacy and intrinsic motivation because developing writers realize that they are capable of improving their skills (Schunk & Swartz, 1993). The greater their sense that strategies are useful and help give them control over their writing, the more likely they will be to make use of them. Strategy use, in turn, will promote skill acquisition (Bandura, 1997; Graham et al., 1995; Schunk, 1989).

Feedback is crucial for writers because it allows them to see the discrepancies between their current performance and their goals. The feedback helps move them from where they are to where they would like to be and provides direction on what strategies to utilize to achieve their goals (Schutz, 1993). Once they isolate discrepancies and their causes through either internal or external feedback, additional strategies or effort can be applied. On simple activities, the response to feedback will most likely be increased effort, which often results in a removal of the discrepancy (Bandura & Cervone, 1983). On complex tasks, however, the response often is to engage in multiple strategies that may not result in narrowing the discrepancy, but instead creates cognitive overload (Cervone, 1993). In the complex task of writing, this can lead to less, not more, productive activities.

Therefore, the most useful feedback on writing will likely involve specific knowledge about how to move toward one's writing goals. Case study research has indicated that students respond favorably to specific and explicit ways to improve their writing (Straub, 1996, 1997); students are quite clear about their need for specific coaching about their writing. In a number of studies examining student response to teacher comments, students responded very well to comments that dealt with organization, development, and matters of form, but resisted comments that dealt with the value of their ideas or issues they did not consider germane to the writing task (Cleary, 1996; Larson, 1995; Straub, 1997). Those providing feedback need to contribute in useful ways to the ongoing process of balancing the writing challenge with the writer's skills and motivations. How readers of student writing choose to make that contribution sends strong signals about who controls the writing process. Students appear to be very aware of control issues in writing and recognize when the person giving feedback begins to exert too much control (Straub, 1996).

Although we strongly believe that developing motivation to write is best conceived of as a process of building intrinsic motivation, rewards may play a productive role. Rewards can help build achievement-directed motivation when they are made contingent on student effort (Brophy, 1987; Stipek & Kowalski, 1989) and on progress in relation to short-term goals (Schunk, 1989). A further positive factor may come when individuals are rewarded for putting a large amount of cognitive or physical effort into writing. The sensation of high effort can acquire secondary reward properties that ameliorate, to some degree, the aversiveness of writing for some students. Reducing the aversiveness through reward may increase young writers' general readiness to expend effort in goal-directed writing tasks (Eisenberger & Cameron, 1996). Of course, the possible negative effects of rewards need to be considered, especially if rewards are offered for engaging in writing tasks without consideration of performance (J. Cameron & Pierce, 1994). This could occur if students were, say, promised tangible rewards simply for engaging in writing.

Directions for future research.   An important area for future research involves attempting to better understand task conditions that support motivational development. For example, how do students' cognitive, linguistic, and self-regulatory abilities affect the kinds of writing tasks that they find motivating? What students find motivating to write about will be highly contextualized, of course, involving some combinations of personal and situational interest, knowledge about the topic, processes by which the writing topic was selected, and the extent to which writing has purposes students consider authentic. Another area for research is examining ways of parsing goals within complex, real-life writing tasks (e.g., see Zimmerman & Kitsantas, 1999). What is the effect, for example, of teachers' carefully framing and systematically revisiting mid- to long-term classroom goals to which a given piece of writing relates? How in fact do students approach complex, multifaceted writing tasks? What kinds of classroom structures and coaching best facilitate steady, stress-free progress toward writing goals and produce the highest quality writing products? Systematic pursuit of answers to questions such as these should lead to better specification of the conditions that develop and maintain motivation to write.

Close examination also is needed of the motivational fluctuations that occur during the writing process as students make decisions in complex writing tasks. We have learned a great deal about writing's cognitive processes from the work of pioneers like Flower, Hayes, Bereiter, and Scardamalia. We now need to more systematically examine motivation-related factors such as writing efficacy, goal setting, and choices about revision during the processes of writing. How does motivation factor into students' beginning conceptions of writing tasks and their later reconceptualizations? Is it true for writing, as the general motivational research implies, that writing tasks conceived of too simply in fact become boring and mechanical? At the other end of the continuum, is Larson's (1995) surmise correct that many young writers exceed their performance capabilities? If so, what are the motivational consequences? And is it also true, as Cervone's (1993) work would indicate, that making too many simultaneous changes in a complex and challenging writing task can result in information overload and overpower the writer's processing capacity? Better identification of the conditions that may produce such effects—based on observing student writing and attitudes in naturalistic settings or experimental conditions—would seem to be very important. Finally, how do successful writers maintain a balance of multiple factors such as their knowledge, skills, interest levels, and writing confidence at the outset, during, and as they near the end of writing tasks? When something must be sacrificed, what is? Again, developmental studies of student writers in natural or simulated settings are likely to help us better understand what we need to pay attention to motivationally.

Cluster 4: Creating a Positive Emotional Environment

Anyone who writes has experienced at least some negative feelings about writing. A considerable number of people de-velop even stronger negative feelings, including writing-related emotional distress and a strong distaste for its processes (Daly, 1985; Madigan et al., 1996). The reasons seem as varied as writers' experiences. Even in the best of circumstances, the conditions under which children begin to write often are far from ideal motivationally. For the novice writer, especially, writing may seem excruciatingly slow and the products, filled with erasures and strikeouts, bleak testimonies to the writer's lack of skill. It may be, as Boice (1994) states, that our productive abilities grow more slowly than our critical ones. What is certain is that novice writers are entering an unfamiliar discourse community with new norms and standards. For many, little in their background has prepared them for functioning well in it. They may initially have only a dim conception of writing's usefulness for helping them achieve their intellectual and social goals. Some may find that writing exposes their knowledge and thinking to an uncomfortable level of scrutiny. With this exposure can come feelings of loss of control and its attendant anxieties (Bandura, 1997), which can be amplified when conditions for successful performance and feedback are unclear.

Even successful writers can get into trouble. They may be hypercritical about their own work. Because of anxiety, they may lapse into procrastination or other unproductive habits, such as impulsively starting to write without gathering the necessary information or writing in unhealthy "binges" (Boice, 1994). As affect turns negative, the natural consequence is that students will begin to avoid writing wherever possible. A cycle can thus begin in which lack of writing leads to lack of writing improvement, resulting in even less inclination to continue. Somehow this cycle must be broken for students to have a chance of experiencing the intrinsic motivation writing can bring. At least four conditions seem promising for creating a positive emotional environment for writing.

An obvious starting point is removing conditions that make writing a negative experience. Structurally, this involves eliminating unnecessary stresses related to writing and trying to ensure that students are engaged in enjoyable, successful writing activities. Larson and his colleagues (Larson, Hecker, & Norem, 1985) found enjoyment of the task of writing to make a qualitative difference in student writing. Hayes and Daiker (1984) found that the single most important principle of response in a writing environment was positive reinforcement. Teachers should spend as much energy on praising good writing as they do in pointing out errors and suggesting improvements. In addition, a safe environment needs to express an openness to all kinds of written and oral self-expression, what Oldfather (1993) has called "honored voice." In such an environment, teachers pay careful attention to what students write and say, and students learn to treat each others' ideas with respect.

Engagement is another component essential to fostering a positive emotional environment. Csikszentmihalyi (1975) defined engagement as a balance between a challenging task and the ability to carry out the task. Wigfield et al. (1998) proposed that the critical components for task involvement are allowing adequate time based on student needs and helping students plan and organize their writing process. Cleary (1991) found that students with teachers who assisted them in breaking down their writing into manageable pieces viewed complex assignments as challenging rather than overwhelming. Children's engagement also has been found to be directly influenced by their perceptions of teacher warmth and interest (Skinner & Belmont, 1993). In classrooms where teachers create a climate of trust, caring, and mutual concern, students are motivated to engage (Connell & Wellborn, 1991; Wentzel, 1997).

A second factor in countering negative attitudes toward writing is giving students a significant measure of control. Several factors likely contribute to feelings of control. Perhaps most basic is knowledge—having something to say. Too often, students are assigned writing tasks on topics where they have little content mastery. Creating a writing problem space (Flower et al., 1990) with diffuse and poorly structured knowledge is unlikely to lead to a successful writing experience. Also, simply having knowledge may motivate writing—as information collections grow, so will interest, organization, and the belief that communicating that information is worthwhile (Boice, 1994). Second, there is growing evidence that writing-strategy training (e.g., Graham & Harris, 1989b, 1993) and building efficacy for using strategies (Schunk & Zimmerman, 1997) strengthen both writing skills and efficacy. As Bandura (1997) pointed out, anxiety decreases as efficacy for a task increases. Third, certain kinds of feedback—especially feedback giving information on progress toward writing goals—appear to enhance student feelings of control (Schunk & Swartz, 1993; Straub, 1996, 1997). Finally, and perhaps most simply, is giving students manageable writing tasks. Major writing tasks can be broken into subtasks, retaining the positive motivational effects of challenge but making the task manageable. Breaking writing tasks into sections also affords students multiple opportunities to revise and improve their work.

Many students' negative attitudes about writing seem to stem from their patterns of self-talk. Interestingly, there is at least some evidence that both attitudes and self-talk are independent of how students actually write and task difficulty (Madigan et al., 1996). No matter what their ability or how easy or hard the writing task, students variously may tell themselves that they aren't capable of writing well, blame themselves for waiting too long to write, consider writing to be a special talent that only others have, compare themselves unfavorably to an unrealistic standard of perfection, or assure themselves they can't begin writing because conditions aren't exactly right.

A large body of research on self-management (see, e.g., Kazdin, 1994) has shown, however, that systematic programs countering negative self-talk can change attitudes and promote positive responses for problems ranging from smoking to poor social skills. The keys to most such programs are monitoring negative thought patterns (e.g., "I don't know how to begin") and systematically substituting positive ones (e.g., "I don't have to start with the introduction. Why don't I just start here and come back to the introduction later?"). Closely related to monitoring negative self-talk is an approach Bandura (1997) proposed for increasing efficacy—helping individuals reinterpret their physiological responses to stress-inducing situations in more positive terms. In writing, this would involve helping students understand their feelings of anxiousness before or during writing as a normal physiological response to a challenging and stimulating task—not as a signal that they are about to fail. Of course, this reframing can complement more direct routes to increasing efficacy—enactive task mastery (i.e., writing successfully), seeing successful models for performance (e.g., by the teacher, by peers, or by looking at other examples of writing), and encouragement.

CONCLUSIONS

Writing is an immensely valuable intellectual and social tool but presents extraordinary motivational challenges. The act of writing is a complex, protracted, problem-solving task in which motivation is critical but difficult to establish and maintain. Writing also represents mysterious new forms of discourse for many children; we often do not do a good job of showing them writing's potential for enhancing their ability to think and communicate. In school, writing's use for evaluative purposes often dominates, with assigned writing and writing on tests taking precedence over writing to share knowledge, points of view, and feelings. Building lasting motivation to write requires careful attention to the conditions under which students write.

We see a number of keys to developing motivation to write, all related to intrinsic motivation. We first need to build student beliefs about writing's nature and potential. These include not only a sense of writing's power, but also a realistic appraisal of its difficulty. Students need to see writing's value as an intellectual and social tool, as well as develop confidence in their writing ability. Second, authentic writing goals and contexts are likely to provide motivational support. Real purposes and audiences clearly convey writing's pragmatic purposes and help students develop a sense of their own writing voice. Third, developing writers need to experience writing task conditions supportive of motivation. These would include encountering complex writing tasks in manageable parts; being helped to set specific, proximal goals; receiving feedback on progress toward goals; and learning writing strategies and when to use them. Fourth, because of writing's complexity and students' prior experiences in many classrooms, many students will have negative feelings about writing and have unproductive writing habits. Approaches are needed that help students deal with negative affect and establish new, productive writing approaches.

Extensive basic and applied research is needed to explicate the factors affecting the development of writing motivation. At least some of this research needs to focus on teachers because of their roles as models for student writing beliefs and feedback providers. Programs for strengthening student writing motivation likely need to start by building teachers' conceptions of the transactional, constructive, problem-solving nature of writing; its intellectual and social utility; and its unique motivational challenges. Teachers' views of writing are very likely to carry over into the design and conduct of their students' writing experiences. Programs that develop student motivation for writing are most likely to be designed and implemented by those who understand, implicitly, the power and pleasure of writing.

REFERENCES

Ames, C. (1992). Classrooms: Goals, structures, and student motivation. *Journal of Educational Psychology, 84,* 261–271.

Ames, C., & Archer, J. (1988). Achievement in the classroom: Student learning strategies and motivational processes. *Journal of Educational Psychology, 80,* 260–267.

Applebee, A. N., & Langer, J. (1984). *Contexts for learning to write: Studies of secondary school instruction.* Norwood, NJ: Ablex.

Bandura, A. (1997). *Self-efficacy: The exercise of control.* New York: Freeman.

Bandura, A., & Cervone, D. (1983). Self-evaluative and self-efficacy mechanisms governing the motivational effects of goal systems. *Journal of Personality and Social Psychology, 45,* 1017–1028.

Benton, S. L., Corkill, A. J., Sharp, J. M., Downey, R. G., & Khramtsova, I. (1995). Knowledge, interest, and narrative writing. *Journal of Educational Psychology, 87,* 66–78.

Bereiter, C., & Scardamalia, M. (1987). *The psychology of written composition.* Hillsdale, NJ: Lawrence Erlbaum Associates, Inc.

Bergin, D., & LaFave, C. (1998). Continuities between motivation research and whole language philosophy of instruction. *Journal of Literacy Research, 30,* 321–356.

Berninger, V. W., Fuller, F., & Whitaker, D. (1996). A process model of writing development across the lifespan. *Educational Psychology Review, 8,* 193–218.

Boice, R. (1994). *How writers journey to comfort and fluency.* Westport, CT: Praeger.

Borkowski, J. G., Weyhing, R. S., & Carr, M. (1988). Effects of attributional retraining on strategy-based reading comprehension of learning-disabled students. *Journal of Educational Psychology, 80,* 46–53.

Brophy, J. (1987). On motivating students. In D. Berliner & B. Rosenshine (Eds.), *Talks to teachers* (pp. 201–245). New York: Random House.

Brown, J., Collins, A., & Duguid, P. (1989). Situated cognition of learning. *Educational Researcher, 18,* 32–42.

Bruning, R., Horn, C., & Sodoro, J. (1998, December). *What readers believe about transactions with texts: A closer look.* Paper presented at the National Reading Conference, Austin, TX.

Bruning, R., & Schweiger, B. (1997). Integrating science and literacy experiences to motivate students learning. In J. T. Guthrie & A. Wigfield (Eds.), *Reading engagement: Motivating readers through integrated instruction* (pp. 149–182). Newark, DE: International Reading Association.

Calfee, R., & Patrick, C. (1995). *Teach our children well.* Stanford, CA: Stanford Alumni Association.

Calkins, L. M. (1994). *The art of teaching writing.* Portsmouth, NH: Heinemann.

Cameron, C. A., Hunt, A. K., & Linton, M. J. (1996). Written expression as recontextualization: Children write in social time. *Educational Psychology Review, 8,* 125–150.

Cameron, J., & Pierce, W. D. (1994). Reinforcement, reward, and intrinsic motivation: A meta-analysis. *Review of Educational Research, 64,* 363–423.

Cervone, D. (1993). The role of self-referent cognitions in goal setting, motivation, and performance. In M. Rabinowitz (Ed.), *Cognitive science foundations of instruction* (pp. 57–95). Hillsdale, NJ: Lawrence Erlbaum Associates, Inc.

Cleary, L. M. (1991). Affect and cognition in the writing processes of eleventh graders. *Written Communication, 8,* 473–507.

Cleary, L. M. (1996). I think I know what my teachers want now: Gender and writing motivation. *English Journal, 85*(1), 50–57.

Codling, R. M., & Gambrell, L. B. (1997). *The motivation to write profile: An assessment tool for elementary teachers.* College Park: University of Maryland.

Connell, J. P., & Wellborn, J. G. (1991). Competence, autonomy, and relatedness: A motivational analysis of self-system processes. In M. R. Gunnar & L. A. Stroufe (Eds.), *Self-processes and development: The Minnesota Symposium and Child Development* (Vol. 23, pp. 43–78). Hillsdale, NJ: Lawrence Erlbaum Associates, Inc.

Corno, L. (1993). The best laid plans: Modern conceptions of volition and educational research. *Educational Researcher, 22*(2), 14–22.

Crystal, D. (1997). *The Cambridge encyclopedia of language.* Cambridge, England: Cambridge University Press.

Csikszentmihalyi, M. (1975). *Beyond boredom and anxiety.* San Francisco: Jossey-Bass.

Csikszentmihalyi, M., & Rathunde, K. (1993). The measurement of flow in everyday life: Toward a theory of emergent motivation. In J. Jacobs (Ed.), *Developmental perspectives on motivation: Nebraska symposium of motivation, 1992* (pp. 57–98). Lincoln: University of Nebraska Press.

Daly, J. A. (1985). Writing apprehension. In M. Rose (Ed.), *When a writer can't write* (pp. 42–82). New York: Guilford.

Deci, E. L., Vallerand, R. J., Pelletier, L. G., & Ryan, R. M. (1991). Motivation and education: The self-determination perspective. *Educational Psychologist, 26,* 325–346.

Doyle, W. (1986). Classroom organization and management. In M. Wittrock (Ed.), *Handbook of research on teaching* (pp. 392–431). New York: Macmillan.

Dweck, C., & Leggett, E. (1988). A social-cognitive approach to motivation and personality. *Psychological Review, 95,* 256–273.

Eisenberger, R., & Cameron, J. (1996). Detrimental effects of reward. *American Psychologist, 51,* 1153–1166.

Elbow, P. (1994). *Landmark essays on voice and writing.* Davis, CA: Hermagoras Press.

Flower, L., & Hayes, J. (1981). Plans that guide the composing process. In C. Frederiksen & J. Dominic (Eds.), *The nature, development and teaching of written communication* (pp. 39–58). Hillsdale, NJ: Lawrence Erlbaum Associates, Inc.

Flower, L., Stein, V., Ackerman, J., Kantz, M. J., McCormick, K., & Peck, W. C. (1990). *Reading-to-write: Exploring a cognitive and social process.* New York: Oxford University Press.

Flower, L., Wallace, D. L., Norris, L., & Burnett, R. A. (1994). *Making thinking visible: Writing, collaborative planning, and classroom inquiry.* Urbana, IL: National Council of Teachers of English.

Graham, S. (1997). Executive control in the revising of students with learning and writing difficulties. *Journal of Educational Psychology, 89,* 223–234.

Graham, S., & Harris, K. R. (1989a). Components analysis of cognitive strategy instruction: Effects on learning disabled students' compositions and self-efficacy. *Journal of Educational Psychology, 81,* 353–361.

Graham, S., & Harris, K. R. (1989b). Improving learning disabled students' skills at composing essays: Self-instructional strategy training. *Exceptional Children, 56,* 210–214.

Graham, S., & Harris, K. R. (1993). Self-regulated strategy development: Helping students with learning problems develop as writers. *Elementary School Journal, 94,* 169–181.

Graham, S., MacArthur, C., & Schwartz, S. (1995). The effects of goal setting and procedural facilitation on the revising behavior and writing performance of students with writing and learning problems. *Journal of Educational Psychology, 87,* 230–240.

Graves, D. H. (1991). *Build a literate classroom.* Portsmouth, NH: Heinemann.

Graves, D. H. (1994). *A fresh look at writing.* Portsmouth, NH: Heinemann.

Guthrie, J. T., & Alao, S. (1997). Designing contexts to increase motivations for reading. *Educational Psychologist, 32,* 95–105.

Guthrie, J. T., & McCann, A. D. (1997). Characteristics of classrooms that promote motivations and strategies for learning. In J. T. Guthrie & A. Wigfield (Eds.), *Reading engagement: Motivating readers through integrated instruction* (pp. 128–148). Newark, DE: International Reading Association.

Hayes, J. R. (1996). *The science of writing.* Mahwah, NJ: Lawrence Erlbaum Associates, Inc.

Hayes, M., & Daiker, D. (1984). Using protocol analysis in evaluating responses to student writing. *Freshman English News, 13,* 1–5.

Hidi, S. (1990). Interest and its contribution as a mental resource for learning. *Review of Educational Research, 60,* 549–571.

Hidi, S., & Anderson, V. (1992). Situational interest and its impact on reading and expository writing. In K. Reinninger, S. Hidi, & A. Krapp (Eds.), *The role of interest in learning and development* (pp. 215–238). Hillsdale, NJ: Lawrence Erlbaum Associates, Inc.

Hiebert, E. H. (1994). Becoming literate through authentic tasks: Evidence and adaptations. In R. B. Ruddell, M. R. Ruddell, & H. Singer (Eds.), *Theoretical models and processes of reading* (pp. 391–413). Newark, DE: International Reading Association.

Kazdin, A. E. (1994). *Behavior modification in applied settings.* Belmont, CA: Brooks/Cole.

Langer, J. A. (1992). *Literature instruction: A focus on student response.* Urbana, IL: National Council of Teachers of English.

Larson, R. (1995). Flow and writing. In M. Csikszentmihalyi & I. S. Csikszentmihalyi (Eds.), *Optimal experience: Psychological studies of flow in consciousness* (pp. 150–171). Cambridge, England: Cambridge University Press.

Larson, R., Hecker, B., & Norem, J. (1985, October/November). Students' experience with research projects: Pains, enjoyment, and success. *High School Journal, 61–69.*

Lepper, M. R., & Hodell, M. (1989). Intrinsic motivation in the classroom. In C. Ames & R. Ames (Eds.), *Research on motivation in education* (pp. 73–105). San Diego, CA: Academic.

Levy, C. M., & Ransdell, S. (1996). *The science of writing: Theories, methods, individual differences, and applications.* Mahwah, NJ: Lawrence Erlbaum Associates, Inc.

Locke, E. A., & Latham, G. P. (1990). *A theory of goal setting and task performance.* Englewood Cliffs, NJ: Prentice Hall.

Madigan, R., Linton, P., & Johnson, S. (1996). The paradox of writing apprehension. In C. M. Levy, & S. Ransdell (Eds.), *The science of writing theories, methods, individual differences, and applications* (pp. 295–307). Mahwah, NJ: Lawrence Erlbaum Associates, Inc.

McCracken, N. M. (1992). *Gender issues and the teaching of writing.* Portsmouth, NH: Heinemann.

Meece, J. L. (1991). The classroom context and students' motivational goals. In M. L. Maehr & P. R. Pintrich (Eds.), *Advances in motivation and achievement* (pp. 261–286). Greenwich, CT: JAI.

Meece, J. L., & Miller, S. D. (1992, April). *Promoting independent literacy skills and motivation to learn in low achieving elementary school students.* Paper presented at the annual meeting of the American Educational Research Association, San Francisco.

Meece, J. L., & Miller, S. D. (1999). Changes in elementary school children's achievement goals for reading and writing: Results of a longitudinal and an intervention study. *Scientific Studies of Reading, 3,* 207–229.

Miller, S. D., Adkins, T., & Hooper, M. L. (1993). Why teachers select specific literacy assignments and students' reactions to them. *Journal of Reading Behavior, 25,* 69–95.

National Center for Education Statistics. (1997). *Report in brief: NAEP 1996 trends in academic progress.* Washington, DC: U.S. Department of Education.

Nicholls, J. G. (1984). Achievement motivation: Conception of ability, subjective experience, task choice, and performance. *Psychological Review, 91,* 328–346.

Oldfather, P. (1993). What students say about motivating experiences in a whole language classroom. *Reading Teacher, 46,* 672–681.

Oldfather, P., & Dahl, K. (1994). Toward a social constructivist reconceptualization of intrinsic motivation for literacy learning. *Journal of Reading Behavior, 26,* 139–158.

Olson, D. R. (1994). *The world on paper: The conceptual and cognitive implications of writing and reading.* Cambridge, England: Cambridge University Press.

Pajares, F., & Johnson, M. J. (1996). Self-efficacy beliefs and the writing performance of entering high school students. *Psychology in the Schools, 33,* 163–175.

Pajares, F., Miller, M. D., & Johnson, M. J. (1999). Gender differences in writing self-beliefs of elementary school students. *Journal of Educational Psychology, 91,* 50–61.

Pajares, F., & Valiante, G. (1997). The predictive and mediational role of the writing self-efficacy beliefs of upper elementary students. *Journal of Educational Research, 90,* 353–360.

Palmquist, M., & Young, R. (1992). The notion of giftedness and student expectations about writing. *Written Communication, 9,* 137–168.

Phillips, D. A., & Zimmerman, M. (1990). The developmental course of perceived competence and incompetence among competent children. In R. J. Sternberg & J. Kolligian (Eds.), *Competence considered* (pp. 41–67). New Haven, CT: Yale University Press.

Pintrich, P. R., & DeGroot, E. V. (1990). Motivational and self-regulated learning components of classroom academic performance. *Journal of Educational Psychology, 82,* 33–40.

Schiwy, M. (1996). *A voice of her own: Women and the journal-writing journey.* New York: Simon & Schuster.

Schraw, G., & Bruning, R. (1996). Readers' implicit models of reading. *Reading Research Quarterly, 31,* 290–305.

Schraw, G., & Bruning, R. (1999). How implicit models of reading affect motivation to read and reading engagement. *Scientific Studies of Reading, 3,* 281–302.

Schunk, D. H. (1989). Learning goals and children's reading comprehension. *Journal of Reading Behavior, 21,* 279–293.

Schunk, D. H. (1991). Goal setting and self-evaluation: A social cognitive perspective on self-regulation. In M. L. Maehr & P. R. Pintrich (Eds.), *Advances in motivation and achievement* (pp. 85–113). Greenwich, CT: JAI.

Schunk, D. H., & Rice, J. M. (1991). Learning goals and progress feedback during reading comprehension instruction. *Journal of Reading Behavior, 23,* 351–364.

Schunk, D. H., & Swartz, C. W. (1993). Goals and progress feedback: Effects on self-efficacy and writing achievement. *Contemporary Educational Psychology, 18,* 337–354.

Schunk, D. H., & Zimmerman, B. (1994). *Self-regulation of learning and performance: Issues and educational applications.* Hillsdale, NJ: Lawrence Erlbaum Associates, Inc.

Schunk, D. H., & Zimmerman, B. J. (1997). Developing self-efficacious readers and writers: The role of social and self-regulatory processes. In J. T. Guthrie & A. Wigfield (Eds.), *Reading engagement: Motivating readers through integrated instruction* (pp. 34–50). Newark, DE: International Reading Association.

Schutz, P. A. (1993). Additional influences on response certitude and feedback requests. *Contemporary Educational Psychology, 18,* 427–441.

Shell, D., Colvin, C., & Bruning, R. (1995). Self-efficacy, attributions, and outcome expectancy mechanisms in reading and writing achievement: Grade-level and achievement-level differences. *Journal of Educational Psychology, 87,* 386–398.

Shell, D., Murphy, C., & Bruning, R. (1989). Self-efficacy and outcome expectancy mechanisms in reading and writing performance. *Journal of Educational Psychology, 81,* 91–100.

Skinner, E. A., & Belmont, M. J. (1993). Motivation in the classroom: Reciprocal effects of teacher behavior and student engagement across the school year. *Journal of Educational Psychology, 85,* 571–581.

Skinner, E. A., Wellborn, J. G., & Connell, J. P. (1990). What it takes to do well in school and whether I've got it: A process model of perceived control and children's engagement and achievement in school. *Journal of Educational Psychology, 82,* 22–32.

Snow, C. E. (1983) Literacy and language: Relationships during the preschool years. *Harvard Educational Review, 53,* 165–187.

Spaulding, C. (1992). The motivation to read and write. In M. Doyle (Ed.), *Reading/writing connections* (pp. 177 201). Newark, DE: International Reading Association.

Stipek, D., & Kowalski, P. (1989). Learned helplessness in task-orienting versus performance-orienting testing conditions. *Journal of Educational Psychology, 81,* 384–391.

Straub, R. (1996). The concept of control in teacher response: Defining the varieties of "directive" and "facilitative" commentary. *College Composition and Communication, 47,* 223–251.

Straub, R. (1997). Students' reactions to teacher comments: An exploratory study. *Research in the Teaching of English, 31,* 91–119.

Turner, J. C. (1995). The influence of classroom contexts on young children's motivation for literacy. *Reading Research Quarterly, 30,* 410–441.

Wentzel, K. R. (1997). Student motivation in middle school: The role of perceived pedagogical caring. *Journal of Educational Psychology, 89,* 411–419.

Wigfield, A., Eccles, J. S., & Rodriguez, D. (1998). The development of children's motivation in school contexts. *Review of Research in Education, 23,* 73–118.

Zimmerman, B. J., & Kitsantas, A. (1999). Acquiring writing revision skill: Shifting from process to outcome self-regulatory goals. *Journal of Educational Psychology, 91,* 241–250.

EDUCATIONAL PSYCHOLOGIST, *35*(1), 39–50

Reading and Writing Relations and Their Development

Jill Fitzgerald

School of Education
University of North Carolina at Chapel Hill

Timothy Shanahan

Department of Curriculum and Instruction
University of Illinois, Chicago

A brief retrospective is first provided on the study of reading and writing relations. Next, it is suggested that research has supported the theoretical contention that reading and writing rely on analogous mental processes and isomorphic knowledge. Four basic types of shared knowledge are delineated. Then, reasons are articulated about why it is also important to consider the separability of reading and writing. Further, over time, as reading and writing are learned, the nature of their relation changes. A description is then offered of a preliminary developmental outlook on the relation of reading and writing. The article concludes with theoretical and practical implications for use of a developmental model.

The history of the separation of reading and writing within American education is well documented (Nelson & Calfee, 1998b), and there have been diverse speculations as to why this segregation has occurred. One explanation is that societies place different values on the attainment of reading and writing (Kaestle, 1985), and if reading is more valued than writing, then there would be an absence of writing instruction. There has also been a political division between reading and writing educators, as different professional organizations have taken responsibility for these two subjects (Clifford, 1989). This means that different groups of educators developed separate curricula, instructional materials, and assessments, despite the relations that may exist between reading and writing. Finally, separation can result from pedagogical, cognitive, and developmental theories that cast reading and writing as mutually irrelevant (Shanahan, 1988).

Theory plays a decisive role in defining constructs and determining where their margins and separations are. For example, developmental readiness theories—in which premature teaching was thought to be ineffective, inefficient, or even harmful—held writing to be dependent on the earlier attainment of reading ability (Gesell, 1925). Schools, in fear of doing harm, delayed writing instruction until reading behaviors were firmly established. Recent advances in cognitive and developmental theory have suggested a very different picture of reading and writing connections, with potentially important epistemological and pedagogical implications.

The research into reading–writing connections has taken three basic approaches (Tierney & Shanahan, 1991): rhetorical relations, procedural connections, and shared knowledge. The rhetorical approach is based on the idea that reading and writing are communications activities and that readers and writers gain insights about how communication works by being both sender and receiver. This work has been well documented recently (Nelson & Calfee, 1998a) and will not be the focus of this article.

The procedural approach treats reading and writing as functional activities that can be combined to accomplish external goals. This approach studies, usually through task analysis, how reading and writing can be used together. These studies have tended to emphasize the combination of reading and writing within academic tasks. These include, for example, explorations of the impact of note taking on comprehension (Slotte & Lanka, 1999), how students synthesize texts when writing reports (Lenski, 1998), or how reading is used in writing revision (Beal, 1996). This approach has not attracted a great deal of research attention, and there is much that could be learned from these types of investigations. This area of investigation is also beyond the scope of this article.

The third approach, the one that has attracted the most research attention and that is the focus of this article, is an analy-

Requests for reprints should be sent to Jill Fitzgerald, University of North Carolina at Chapel Hill, Peabody Hall CB 3500, Chapel Hill, NC 27599–3500. E-mail: jfitzger@email.unc.edu

sis of the shared knowledge and cognitive processes between reading and writing. Such research begins with the premise that reading and writing are constellations of cognitive processes that depend on knowledge representations at various linguistic levels (phonemic, orthographic, semantic, syntactic, pragmatic). Reading and writing are connected, according to such views, because they depend on identical or similar knowledge representations, cognitive processes, and contexts and contextual constraints. Therefore, we should expect reading and writing to be quite similar, their developments should parallel each other closely, and some type of pedagogical combination may be useful in making learning more efficient. This idea of common or shared knowledge or process has been explored for several decades, though often with the theory more implied than stated. Researchers sought correlations among measures of reading and writing, and these connections were often put forth as evidence that reading and writing could be taught better or that they reflected common cognitive resources underlying reading and writing. As the "cognitive revolution" proceeded, and the notion of active learners or active readers became more widely held, the metaphor of a reader composing a text in his or her mind encouraged greater attention to the cognitive and linguistic similarities of reading and writing (Tierney & Pearson, 1983) and to intensified efforts to pursue such correlations.

SHARED KNOWLEDGE IN READING AND WRITING

So what knowledge may we expect readers and writers to hold in common? Research has focused on four basic types of knowledge (see Table 1; basic types of knowledge are in bold) that both readers and writers must use (Fitzgerald, 1990, 1992). One superordinate kind of knowledge is *metaknowledge,* which includes pragmatics. Research has clearly shown that reading and writing entail metacognitive and pragmatic knowledge (Langer, 1986; Shell, Colvin, & Bruning, 1995). Metaknowledge refers to several subcategories of knowledge, including knowing about the functions and purposes of reading and writing; knowing that readers and writers interact; monitoring one's own meaning-making (metacomprehension) and monitoring word identification or production strategies; and monitoring one's own knowledge. The metacognitive aspect of reading and writing includes motivational factors such as expectations for success.

A second kind of superordinate knowledge is *domain knowledge about substance and content.* This refers to all knowledge or awareness that readers and writers have, no matter what the source. This category includes what is often referred to as "world knowledge" or "prior knowledge" (the knowledge a reader brings to a text), but it also includes the knowledge that can result from a reading or writing interaction. Domain knowledge has to do with the subcategories of semantics or meaning, including word meanings and the

meanings or ideas that are constructed through the context of connected text.

A third kind of superordinate knowledge is *knowledge about universal text attributes.* Issues of shared text knowledge have generated the greatest research attention within studies of reading–writing relations. This area includes three subcategories, each with two or more kinds of knowledge. First, there is graphophonics, or letter and word identification and generation, including phonological awareness, grapheme awareness, and morphology. Readers, to read words, must learn to deal with letters and phonemes and how they combine. Writers, likewise, must learn about letters and sounds if they are to spell accurately. To know graphophonics, readers and writers must develop both phonological awareness (the ability to perceive and manipulate separate words, word parts, and individual phonemes or sounds within words) and the ability to perceive and discriminate letter shapes and various typographical representations such as punctuation.

A second subcategory of text attributes is syntax: the rules or grammar for constructing sentences and for using punctuation (Kellogg, 1994). Readers and writers must learn to recognize and produce meaningful syntactic orderings of words and how to use punctuation. Although syntactic knowledge can be drawn from oral language, some syntactic structures are only commonly found in text and those, consequently, must be learned from reading.

The third subcategory of text attributes is another form of syntax that we call text format, which includes syntax of larger chunks of text, such as story grammars, and more general forms of text organization such as graphics (Shanahan, 1984). This includes a wide range of information such as understanding of the relations between pictures and print, directionality, structural organization of text, or formatting features such as paragraphing, graphical structuring, and so on.

A fourth kind of superordinate knowledge is *procedural knowledge and skill to negotiate reading and writing* (Langer, 1986). This refers to knowing how to access, use, and generate knowledge in any of the areas previously mentioned, as well as the ability to instantiate smooth integration of various processes. Procedural knowledge can include both relatively automatic processes such as anticipation or recalling relevant information from memory, as well as intentional strategies such as prediction, questioning, or trying to find analogies (Kellogg, 1994).

Note that Table 1 shows how the knowledge categories are linked to the four generic superordinate categories that represent the most common divisions of oral language research and theory, namely, pragmatics, semantics, phonology (here referred to as graphophonics, because literacy also has a grapheme component), and syntactics. These are represented in Table 1 in italics.

Each of the four superordinate categories has attracted attention from researchers, and each is associated with a collection of correlation coefficients measuring the relations among

TABLE 1
Categories of Knowledge That Readers and Writers Use

- **Metaknowledge (*Pragmatics*)**
  Knowing about functions and purposes of reading and writing
  Knowing that readers and writers interact
  Monitoring one's own meaning making (metacomprehension) and word identification or production strategies
  Monitoring one's own knowledge
- **Domain knowledge about substance and content (prior knowledge, content knowledge gained while reading and writing)**
  Semantics
    Vocabulary meaning
    Meaning created through context of connected text
- **Knowledge about universal text attributes**
  Graphophonics—Letter and word identification and generation
    Phonological awareness
    Grapheme awareness (letter shapes, knowledge of typographical representations such as punctuation and capitalization)
    Morphology (word structure and orthographic patterns)
  Syntax
    Syntax of sentences
    Punctuation
  Text format
    Syntax of larger chunks of text (e.g., story grammars and expository text structures)
    Text organization (e.g., sequence of text, graphics)
- **Procedural knowledge and skill to negotiate reading and writing**
  Knowing how to access, use, and generate knowledge in any of the previous areas
  Instantiating smooth integration of various processes

Note. Items in bold represent basic types of knowledge. Items in italics represent the most common divisions of oral language research and theory.

particular reading and writing variables. The evidence for shared knowledge takes a variety of forms, and there are several extensive reviews of this literature or, more properly, these literatures (see, e.g., Nelson & Calfee, 1998a; Reuter, 1993; Shanahan & Tierney, 1990; Stotsky, 1983; Tierney & Shanahan, 1991). Given these extensive reviews, we offer only illustrative examples, rather than a comprehensive analysis, of each of the approaches to the study of shared knowledge perspectives of reading–writing relations.

By far the most popular approach has been to measure correlations across reading and writing within a specific knowledge area. The researcher typically has selected one variable from writing and one from reading and then combined these statistically to discern the pattern. So, for instance, the researcher may measure syntactic complexity in children's writing, or the sophistication of vocabulary, or the accuracy of spelling. Then some measure of reading is taken from the same children. The reading measures have sometimes been specific, such as a particular test of decoding, but more often generalized measures of reading—such as standardized achievement test scores have been used. Then these two sets of scores are correlated to see how closely connected the two measures are.

The basic idea here is that the larger the correlation across reading and writing, the more similar the knowledge in the two areas. Such studies—and there are a large number of these dating back to the 1930s—have usually resulted in moderate correlations, most often in the .20 to .50 range, with occasional correlations above this range (Tierney & Shanahan, 1991). When using measures without ceiling or floor effects, the magnitudes of these correlations have been fairly consistent, no matter what the age or grade levels of the participants or the nature of the specific measurements. What this means is that in most of these studies reading and writing have typically explained no more than 25% of the variance in each other. The low correlations have often been blamed on the low reliability of the writing measures or explained by the partial nature of the approach taken. Given that only spelling or only vocabulary or only some other single aspect of writing has usually been considered, it is possible that much of the relation between reading and writing would be missed by any given study. Most of these studies have been small scale (fewer than 50 participants), have been conducted at a single point in time (few longitudinal or cross-panel studies), and have usually focused on bivariate relations as opposed to multivariate relations. Consequently, the results of such studies are more provocative than informative, as they are unable to address issues of covariance or development, and their generalizability is often questionable.

However, there has been a handful of studies that have taken more complex looks at multiple reading and writing variables or that have considered the relations longitudinally or through multigrade cross-panel designs (e.g., Langer, 1986; Loban, 1976; Shanahan, 1984). Even with these, however, it is always possible that the measures correlate with common moderator variables such as IQ or language ability. Given the central role that such variables play in both reading and writing—and the high correlation of these with both—it makes little sense conceptually to try to covary their effects from a reading–writing connection. To do so would leave little reliable variance to connect to anything and likely would provide a misleading picture of how instruction could best exploit reading and writing connections. Thus, correlations indicate the existence of a relation of some type but by themselves cannot indicate how to take pedagogical advantage of the shared knowledge of reading and writing.

The purpose of calculating these correlations often has been no more than to speculate on the nature of the connection between reading and writing. But various studies have had other, more immediately practical purposes, such as using young children's writing behaviors to predict beginning reading success (Tymms, 1999), or to try to determine the patterns of instructional needs of college students (Aydelott, 1998) or adult literacy students (Perin, 1998). Because of the consistent, low-to-moderate correlations between reading and writing, it is possible to use measures of either to predict and plan for instruction, to some limited extent, in the other.

More complex correlational approaches are possible too. Shanahan and Lomax (1986, 1988) conducted a series of LISREL analyses of alternative models of reading–writing relations. LISREL allows issues such as directionality to be considered, something precluded in simple correlational analyses, and it supports the evaluation of various explanatory models. So, for example, they were able to consider whether the major interconnections could be summarized best by a model in which reading influenced writing, or one in which writing influenced reading. Their analysis indicated that what they labeled the "interactive model" was most consistent with the extensive collection of reading and writing measures that they had taken on more than 500 children. In their interactive model, reading and writing influenced each other, suggesting a more dynamic relation, with knowledge arising from either reading or writing but then being generalized or diffused to the other process. They also found that the specific patterns of relation changed, with word recognition–spelling connections being relatively more important (as proportion of the variance) early on, but more structural aspects of text knowledge coming into prominence with older or more proficient readers. This model did not consider either procedural or metacognitive relations, however. Given the better fit of the interactive model, these researchers concluded that it was important to teach reading and writing simultaneously, if not together, to gain the greatest efficiency of learning.

A second approach is to examine patterns of relations that exist among analogous aspects of reading and writing knowledge and external variables. The idea here is that if the patterns of relation among reading and writing and other variables are the same, then reading and writing themselves must be quite similar. These studies typically show that reading and writing (including spelling) achievement are more closely related to each other than they are to achievement in other academic areas, or that instructional or social experiences influence reading and writing in similar ways (Pascarella, Edison, Nora, Hagedorn, & Terenzini, 1998;

Wharton-McDonald, Pressley, & Hampton, 1998). Differences can emerge from these types of studies too. For example, in an innovative study of the influence of observation on learning, Couzijn (1999) found that certain types of observation of writing models had differential impacts on reading and writing and that such experiences resulted in somewhat greater transfer of skills in reading. Nevertheless, the differences were small. The results of such studies can also be affected by common moderator variables, though when both correlational and analogous relation evidence are taken together, their results are more persuasive.

Finally, researchers have experimentally intervened, teaching some aspect of either reading or writing in the hopes of engendering a change in both processes. For example, Clarke (1988) set up a program in which first graders wrote using invented spelling and improved their word recognition skills. In another study, guided writing activities were used successfully to increase children's word recognition skills (Santa & Hoien, 1999). Sentence-combining activities in writing have been found to improve sentence-level (but not discourse-level) reading comprehension (Straw & Schreiner, 1982). The conclusion from such studies is that reading or writing knowledge is transferred to the other process, or that reading or writing, because of their similarities, provide especially useful cognitive support for learning the other process.

Taken together, these three kinds of studies provide persuasive evidence that reading and writing rely on corresponding or correlated mental processes and isomorphic knowledge, though the nature of the relations between reading and writing is different at different age or grade levels. The closest correlations between them are best summarized by the aspects of learning that are particularly important or most variant at a given stage of development (such as phonological–orthographic development in the early stages of literacy learning). This suggests that reading and writing may be taught more effectively or efficiently together rather than delaying writing instruction until reading development is completed, as was the historical approach in American education.

READING AND WRITING
ARE DIFFERENT

That reading and writing are closely correlated is beyond dispute, but it is important to note that the correlations between reading and writing are far from perfect. As connected as reading and writing are, they are also cognitively quite separate. Not only can they be learned separately, but even with large numbers of variables (Shanahan, 1984), the amount of shared variance between reading and writing was never found to be more than about .50. Although this is a substantially closer connection than was typically identified in bivariate studies, it is far lower than the unities often presumed by researchers and theoreticians. Given the great amount of shared covariance among different measures of reading and writing, it is doubtful that appreciably higher correlations will result from the inclusion of still more measurements.

Furthermore, studies have examined the use of particular types of knowledge within reading and writing by various groups, including individuals with brain injuries, to see if knowledge use is separable (Beaton, Guest, & Ved, 1997; Boget & Marcos, 1997; Chan, 1992; Niemi, Poskiparta, Vaurus, & Maeki, 1998). Such studies have identified individuals who could read but not write, or who could write a message but not read it themselves. Stotsky (1983) and Tierney (1983) successfully identified groups of good readers–good writers, poor readers–poor writers, good readers–poor writers, and good writers–poor readers. Similar work has been done with reading and spelling (Frith, 1980). The existence of brain injuries that differentially impair reading or writing, or of students who can—for no discernible reason—read well and write poorly or vice versa, suggests the separability of reading and writing processes. What are we to conclude from such evidence? Closer inspections of reading–writing connections reveal important reasons why reading and writing are as separate as they are similar. Langer (1986), in her analyses of multiple procedural and metacognitive variables, concluded that reading and writing were highly similar but that the different cognitive starting points inherent in each prevented them from being more closely aligned. For example, the author's words constrain the meaning-making choices of the reader, but writers have fewer constraints and, thus, must learn to select from a broader array of options. Even more persuasive are close analyses of spelling and word recognition (Cronnell, 1970; Ehri, 1997). If one conceptualizes a sound–symbol relation as a series of connections among letters or letter combinations and alternative pronunciations, it becomes clear that it matters whether one begins with a phoneme or a grapheme. For example, take the /sh/ sound. This phoneme is spelled in a variety of ways in English, including *ch (chantey), s (sure), sh (ship), si (decision),* and *ti (nation).* A writer, starting with the phoneme /sh/, must choose among these five spelling options to write the word properly, whereas a reader, who starts from the letter combination *sh,* only has a single phoneme to choose from. Moving from reading to writing or from writing to reading is not like reversing directions on the same road. The differences in functional starting points can be enough to require different roads altogether. Consequently, reading is a somewhat easier task than writing, and reliance on identical memories would be insufficient to make reading and writing identical processes.

It turns out that this separability is as important as the close connections between reading and writing (Shanahan, 1988). If reading and writing really were identical and not just similar, then it may make sense to teach only reading or writing. Everything learned in one would automatically transfer to the other, so there would be no reason for the double instruction. Historically, reading and writing were taught as if everything, or nearly everything, that was needed for writing achievement could be learned through reading alone. Because this is not the case—reading and writing are only partially correlated—it is necessary to provide separate instruction and experience in each, though various combinations can be valuable for taking advantage of the overlaps.

Interestingly, the cognitive separability of reading and writing may be one reason why they can be combined so effectively to support critical thinking (Tierney, Soter, O'Flahavan, & McGinley, 1989). Reading and writing encourage different enough cognitive operations that they offer alternative perspectives that can give rise to new learning or appreciation. Writing about a text, for example, leads to different types of rethinking than rereading alone provides. If reading and writing were identical, this would not be the case, and if they were very separate, they may not be so mutually supportive.

READING–WRITING RELATIONS AT DIFFERENT DEVELOPMENTAL STAGES

A logical way to explore the relation between reading and writing at different developmental levels is to examine the developmental stages of reading, developmental stages of writing, and theoretical models of the reciprocity of reading and writing at different levels of proficiency. Chall (1996) proposed broad developmental stages of reading, spanning birth through adulthood. However, work in the other two areas is scant. Although some authorities have formulated theories of writing and these sometimes had developmental components (Bereiter & Scardamalia, 1987; Flower, 1994; King & Rentel, 1979), we could locate no broad and comprehensive stage theory of writing development covering a wide range of levels or areas of growth. Further, very little theoretical or empirical work has been done to examine the ways in which reading and writing are related across different developmental levels.

We do know that critical features of learning about reading or writing vary from one developmental level to another. Prior research supports this contention. For example, Shanahan (1984) found that as elementary-age readers became more proficient, their knowledge of sophisticated vocabulary and story structure was increasingly implicated in writing achievement. But few researchers and theoreticians have taken on the project of sketching a broad view of reading–writing relations across proficiency levels.

In this section, we suggest that it is possible to build a preliminary developmental model, covering a wide age span, that describes critical cognitive features or markers that are likely to be important to both reading and writing proficiency at different stages. The sources for our model include the interactive model of reading and writing described earlier (Shanahan & Lomax, 1986, 1988), the list of common categories of knowledge used by readers and writers also described earlier (Fitzgerald, 1990, 1992), and Chall's (1996) stages of reading development.

Critical Knowledge at Various Stages of Reading and Writing

As a preface to this discussion, it is important to note that we are talking only about the features that are common to both reading and writing at each stage. This does not imply that features unique to reading or writing at any given stage are unimportant. Rather, in this preliminary model we simply do not address these features. We take this approach because evidence supporting the commonalties is considerable, and we believe that it is, therefore, appropriate to begin building a model around them. Also, at this date, there is far less research evidence to permit even a cursory analysis of how reading and writing diverge at the various stages. It is evident that at least some of the differences between reading and writing are due to their different purposes and points of departure. For instance, one process begins with the author's words and the other with the writer's ideas, and these different starting points present different cognitive alternatives, memory search problems, and so on. Thus, sorting out the actual differences is likely to require a more thorough task analysis of various kinds of reading and writing—a process beyond the scope of this article and beyond most previous research.

Further, the model highlights and emphasizes the critical features at a given stage. These features are the types of knowledge that are most representative of the learning that occurs at the stages. Again, we are not implying that other features of knowledge are unimportant. Rather, by pointing to the critical understandings of various stages, we see more clearly the differences in stages that should contribute to future theory building.

Our model of critical markers of stages of literacy development is shown in Table 2. In each of the following sections, we begin with a general description of a particular stage. Then we delineate the critical markers of the stage, discussing the markers as they are ordered in Table 2.

It will likely facilitate reading of the following section if readers understand that the critical markers shown in Table 2 are all taken directly from the categories shown in Table 1 that were discussed earlier. Essentially, the superordinate headings and subheadings in Table 1 provide the organizing plan for both the outline given in Table 2 and the discussion that follows. The superordinate headings are noted with bullets and are in bold. Within each stage, the order of markers directly corresponds to the category order in Table 1. In most of the stages, all four of the superordinate categories from Table 1 appear. However, the specific critical features within these superordinate categories vary considerably from stage to stage.

To understand the critical marker stage model we developed, it is also essential to know two things. First, the continuing importance of the four superordinate kinds of knowledge is a reflection of aspects of the relation between reading and writing that is constant over time. That is, these superordinate categories of understandings common to both reading and writing continue to be important throughout the development of literacy.

However, it is also essential to know that, to a large extent, the model is an initial, and very preliminary, attempt to highlight the notion that the nature of the relation between reading and writing may also change over time. This change is evident by comparing the critical subcategories across stages. For example, note that the superordinate category knowledge about universal text attributes occurs in Table 2 in all of the first five stages. However, within this superordinate category, the critical subordinate understandings about universal text attributes change from one stage to the next. For instance, within knowledge about universal text attributes, at Stage 1, the graphophonic knowledge, phonological awareness, and grapheme awareness are critical. By Stage 3, higher level graphophonic knowledge and, more specifically, understanding the morphology of bigger words becomes the critical feature. By Stage 5, within knowledge about universal text attributes, the critical subcategory becomes knowledge of text structure.

Similarly, developmental changes are noted across stages in specific areas of knowledge within other superordinate categories. These changes likewise illustrate that the nature of what is critical in the reading–writing relation changes over time. In other words, there is not a simple explanation of the changing nature of the relation between reading and writing, except to say that the specific (or subcategory) literacy knowledge variables that are critical at one stage are different at another.

Finally, this model is meant to be descriptive of proficient reading and writing development at any given level. Students who struggle with reading and writing are most likely to become unbalanced in their development of reading and writing knowledge, showing lags or deficiencies in some areas and proficiency and growth in others. Although this model is a poor description of the development of many struggling readers and writers, it can help us to think about the needs of poor readers and writers because it identifies areas of essential learning that could be used to plan assessments and instructional interventions for these children. Because of its dual emphasis on reading and writing, it also could highlight areas of strength in written language learning for these children that could be used to support achievement in weaker areas.

Stage 1: Literacy roots.   Both researchers and practitioners commonly refer to this stage as the emergent literacy period. As Chall (1996) said

> From birth until the beginning of formal education, children living in a literate culture with an alphabetic writing system

TABLE 2
Critical Knowledge at Various Stages of Reading and Writing

Stage 1. Literacy Roots (Birth–Age 6)

- **Metaknowledge**: knowing about functions and purposes of reading and writing
- **Domain knowledge about substance and content (developing knowledge of the world)**
- **Knowledge about universal text attributes**
  Graphophonics:
    Phonological awareness
    Grapheme awareness
- **Procedural knowledge**
  Concepts of book

Stage 2: Initial Literacy (Grades 1–2, Ages 6–7)

- **Metaknowledge**
  Knowing that readers and writers interact
  Monitoring for meaning
  Monitoring word making
- **Knowledge about universal text attributes**
  Graphophonics: Letter and word "making"
    Grapheme awareness
    Morphology
  Syntax of sentences
- **Procedural knowledge:** How to use strategies to read and write words

Stage 3: Confirmation, Fluency, Ungluing From Print (Grades 2–3, Ages 7–8)

- **Knowledge about universal text attributes**
  Higher level *Graphophonics*:
    Morphology: Big words
- **Procedural knowledge**
  Instantiating smooth integration of all strategies and processes
  How to "make" big words

Stage 4: Reading and Writing for Learning the New: A First Step (Grades 4–8, Ages 9–13)

- **Metaknowledge**: Metacomprehension
- **Domain knowledge about substance and content** (prior knowledge; using reading and writing to learn)
  Semantics
    Vocabulary meaning
    Meaning created through context of connected text
- **Knowledge about universal text attributes**
  Syntax
    Of sentences
    Of larger chunks of text (e.g., text structures)
- **Procedural knowledge and skill**
  Knowing how to create and use word meanings
  Knowing how to create and use meaningful connected text

Stage 5: Multiple Viewpoints (High School, Ages 14–18)

- **Metaknowledge**: Metacomprehension
- **Domain knowledge about substance and content**
  Semantics
    Vocabulary meaning
    Meaning created through context of connected text
- **Knowledge about universal text attributes**
  Syntax of chunks of text (e.g., text structure)
- **Procedural knowledge and skill**
  Knowing how to see from another's viewpoint
  Knowing how to analyze and critique

Stage 6: Construction and Reconstruction–A Worldview (College, Age 18 and Above)

- **Metaknowledge**, especially knowing about how readers and writers interact
- **Domain knowledge about substance and content**
- **Procedural knowledge and skill**
  Knowing how to see from the viewpoints of others
  Knowing how to analyze and critique

Note. The superordinate headings are represented by bullets and are in bold. Subordinate headings are in italics.

accumulate a fund of knowledge about letters, words, and books. The children grow in their control over various aspects of language—syntax and words. And they gain some insights into the nature of words: that some sound the same at their ends or beginnings (rhyme and alliteration), that they can be broken into parts, and that the parts can be put together (synthesized, blended) to form whole words. (p. 13)

The critical kinds of knowledge developed during this stage are: metaknowledge, knowing about functions and purposes of reading and writing; domain or content knowledge of a wide array of subjects; knowledge of universal text attributes, specifically graphophonic knowledge (phonological knowledge and graphemic knowledge); and procedural knowledge, in which children learn what texts are and how to manipulate them. Research has documented that literate knowledge in this period develops concomitantly in reading, writing, listening, and speaking (Teale & Sulzby, 1986).

Research has also documented that one of the most critical features in the latter part of this stage is phonological awareness (Adams, 1990). However, though the ability to hear and manipulate separate words, parts in words, and sounds in words is critical to literacy development, research indicates that these skills can develop as a result of reading and writing growth (Adams, 1990; Tunmer & Nesdale, 1985) and that they, thus, are not necessarily precursors of literacy development.

Stage 2: Initial literacy.   In Chall's (1996, pp. 15–16) words, the essential aspect of Stage 2 is "learning the arbitrary set of letters and associating these with the corresponding parts of spoken words."

Metaknowledge continues to be a key, but of a different sort in this stage than in Stage 1. Here, students are learning increasingly that readers and writers work together—that is, each works on the premises of the other (Nystrand, 1989). Further, they learn about self-monitoring of their own meaning and word making. For example, monitoring strategies such as asking, "Does this make sense?" are essential for word reading and production (Clay, 1993).

Key knowledge about text attributes is immeasurably important in this period. During this time, students are acquiring grapheme awareness and learning orthographic or morphological patterns in words. They also are learning that (a) their knowledge of syntactically acceptable word orders learned previously through oral language applies in reading and writing and (b) their understandings of acceptable word order can be used to help make sound attempts at new words as they read and write. Finally, they begin to develop procedural knowledge such as using strategic searches and learning to select and produce graphic and syntactic cues, for example, to read and write words and sentences (Clay, 1993; Schwartz, 1997).

Stage 2 can be broken into yet smaller stages. For example, Gentry and Gillet (1993) identified the following spelling periods, which mark cognitive turns in knowing about words:

1. The precommunication stage of writing, in which children make nonalphabetic markings in the belief that this is writing.

2. The semiphonetic stage, in which spellers show that they recognize that letters stand for sounds, though they can only partially represent this knowledge.

3. The phonetic stage, when writers can represent all sounds phonetically, spelling what they hear systematically, though some letter choices do not conform to conventional spelling.

4. The transitional stage, where writers recognize that words have particular "looks" or morphological structures, not just phonological features. For example, children who begin to realize that some words have silent letters may write words such as "haev" for "have," and "supe" for "soup."

5. The conventional stage, in which spellers show greater knowledge of the orthographic system and how it works. Conventional spelling is more likely to emerge in the following reading and writing stage—Stage 3.

Stage 3: Confirmation, fluency, ungluing from print.   The learner in this stage consolidates what was learned earlier, and knowledge access and use becomes more fluent or automatic. Many words can be read at sight and written at will. Several strategies have been developed for reading and writing words and sentences. In short, the reading and writing of words continues to be important, but now the critical ability is procedural, that is, instantiation of smooth integration of various strategies and processes. The major effort during this stage is to make the knowledge that has already been gained more internalized, less deliberate, and less overt. In this way, students are becoming "unglued" from print (Chall, 1996).

At the same time, later in this period, there is a transition into more strenuous efforts to use bigger words. Students now confront texts that present words with more complex orthographic patterns as well as more difficult multisyllabic words. Consequently, of secondary importance during Stage 3, learners are increasingly developing knowledge about specific text attributes, that is, higher level graphophonics, especially focusing on the morphological or orthographic patterns found in complex words.

Stage 4: Reading and writing for learning the new: A first step.   Meaning is the focus of reading and writing at every stage, but beginning at Stage 4, there is a dramatic turn away from the work of linking speech and print. At the beginning of Stage 4, readers and writers focus more deeply on the understanding and interpretation of ideas and thoughts, and, for the first time, reading and writing start to compete with other means of knowing and learning. Research has long supported the contention that around fourth grade, there is a dramatic increase in the academic, abstract words that appear in books, and there is a higher proportion of long and complex sentences (Klare, 1974–1975).

Consequently, of critical importance at Stage 4 are the following. First, metaknowledge or metacomprehension, the self-monitoring of one's own knowledge during reading and writing, is clearly an important feature. Second, knowledge about content, especially the application of prior knowledge, is essential. An equally important aspect of content knowledge is the developing capacity to use both reading and writing to learn new ideas, and, related to content knowledge, readers and writers are learning new vocabulary. Third, a significant area of development entails an increased emphasis on learning about text attributes, that is, learning about more complicated syntactical structures and organizational structures within texts. Reading and writing at previous stages tend to focus on narratives, but now informational texts become increasingly important while knowledge about narrative text structures becomes elaborated. Finally, the procedural knowledge that is critical during this stage entails knowing how to create and use word meanings and knowing how to create and use meaningful connected texts for a variety of purposes.

Stage 5: Multiple viewpoints.
The essential characteristic of Stage 5 is that it involves "dealing with more than one point of view" (Chall, 1996, p. 23). At the same time, many of the essential features of Stage 4 continue to develop and become elaborated throughout Stage 5.

The kinds of knowledge that are pivotal in Stage 5 include metaknowledge, especially metacomprehension and self-monitoring. Higher level awareness of one's own comprehension and meaning production become increasingly important as the ability to create and understand embedded meanings develops. Second, content knowledge for word meanings and more generally for meaning created through connected text, as well as background knowledge, continues to be tremendously important. Third, as reading and writing become more complex, there is continuing development of knowledge about text attributes. Extending from the previous stage, enriched understandings of text structures and realizing how to use them to particular effects grows in importance.

Finally, in the area of procedural knowledge, knowing how to see from another's viewpoint and how to analyze and critique while reading and writing emerge as essential components of development. These procedural critical markers revolve around development of critical thinking. Critical thinking in reading and writing are likely to be reciprocal processes commonly known as critical reading and revision in writing (Fitzgerald, 1989). Critical reading refers to the criticism of one's own thinking and the writer's thinking during reading (cf. Erickson, Hubler, Bean, Smith, & McKenzie, 1987). Revision means making changes at any point in the writing process (Faigley & Witte, 1981). To read and write critically, individuals must use a common critical-thinking process. That is, they must consider compatibilities across au-

thor's and reader's goals, intentions, and beliefs about the piece being read or written. A writer compares his or her own goals and beliefs to what the reader may be expecting, and when there is dissonance, the author makes decisions about alternatives. Similarly, when a reader disagrees with an author's content, the reader must consider alternatives to what the author is saying. When an author decides he or she has written something that a reader will not understand, alternative ways of writing that part must be considered. A final result of revision in writing is that an author may invoke some change during composing to increase the possibility of compatibility across author's and reader's intentions or beliefs. Although critical readers do not change the printed text, they may change their understanding of it or their own goals, beliefs, and expectations. Critical reading and revision in writing both entail dissonance, location, and resolution.

Stage 6: Construction and reconstruction—A worldview.
Chall's (1996) conceptualization of what we are calling Stage 6 originated in Perry's (1970) study of intellectual development during the college years. Perry hypothesized a developmental turn during this most mature stage in which individuals move from a conception of knowledge as factual "rightness" to the conception of knowledge as a more subjective or "qualitative assessment of contextual observations and relationships" (p. 210). The essence of this stage is that individuals develop an increased capacity to construct knowledge by reading and writing through deeper analysis, synthesis, and application of personal judgment. Simultaneously, an increased understanding of reading and writing for specific purposes develops. Readers and writers know better what to skip, what to put in, and what to leave out. Understandings such as these arise from a growing knowledge of what it means for readers to read on the premises of the author and writers to write on the premises of the reader (Nystrand, 1989).

The pivotal kinds of knowledge in Stage 6 include metaknowledge, especially knowledge about how readers and writers interact, and content knowledge, which allows increasing depth of understanding when applied to problems of reading and writing. Procedural knowledge is critical, especially for knowing how to see from others' viewpoints and knowing how to analyze, synthesize, and critique.

IMPLICATIONS

Several implications arise from a critical knowledge model of what is shared in the development of reading and writing. One overarching implication of the model is that rather than separately focusing on a student's reading and writing skills, researchers and educators should focus on the critical shared thinking that underlies both reading and writing. This does not mean that differences between reading and writing should be overlooked. However, because shared variance between reading and writing is relatively great, specific instructional attention to what is different would likely be secondary to instruction intended to develop the common critical thinking. Recent inventories of essential literacy cognitions (Burns, Griffin, & Snow, 1999; New Standards Primary Literacy Standards Committee, 1999) have considered both reading and writing, but they have done this separately. This approach encourages unnecessary, and perhaps inefficient, instructional separations and may lead to unnecessary and potentially misleading duplications of effort by reading and writing researchers. For example, if a cognitive ability such as phonemic segmentation underlies both reading and writing, it would be worthwhile for researchers to consider the impact of phonemic awareness interventions on both reading and writing simultaneously. Similarly, studies of more general interventions, such as reading aloud to children or playing rhyming games with them, are likely to have implications for both reading and writing. Research agendas that consider both types of implication are more likely to lead to complete understandings of such procedures. Such studies may better explain the complexity of children's written language learning as well. Many studies have shown the impact of phonemic awareness training on children's early reading ability, but they have rarely addressed how these procedures influence writing and spelling—or how such training could enable children to draw greater reading knowledge from their early writing experiences, if such an interaction exists.

A second implication results from the developmental focus of this model. The nature of the types of knowledge that are critically important to both reading and writing changes according to a student's developmental level. Consequently, the model implies that assessment should revolve around the critical cognitions highlighted at each stage to locate a given child's developmental level of literacy thinking. It is essential that researchers keep developmental issues clearly in mind when interpreting literacy research as well. For example, at beginning levels of literacy development, phonics instruction has been identified as an important variable in improving reading and spelling achievement (Adams, 1990). However, by fourth grade, the correlation between amount of phonics instruction and reading achievement would be negative. Without a developmental perspective, it would be possible to misinterpret such a correlation as indicating phonics instruction to be a potential problem, rather than a developmental confound. Teachers tend to provide continued phonics instruction to the lowest readers at this point in development, and thus the peculiar and misleading correlation.

Students in any classroom are likely to be at a variety of stages of literacy development, and teachers would be helped by assessment systems that locate children within these stages and identify their functioning with particular areas of learning. Targeting instruction on what children are struggling with cognitively in reading and writing should make that instruction more powerful. How instruction should match cognition has been a matter of much speculation but

not much empirical study (Bear, Invernizzi, Templeton, & Johnston, 1996; Ferroli & Shanahan, 1987; Wood, Bruner, & Ross, 1976). Research needs to consider issues such as whether instruction should try to lead cognition by causing particular types of dissonance or whether it should match cognition to support consolidation of learning.

Research into the connection of instruction and learning will profit by considering the separations of reading and writing as well. Because recognition and production are so cognitively different, it becomes possible to consider the role of different types of practice or experience on learning or to consider the immediacy, or lack of immediacy, of training transfer. Psychologists could help engineer more powerful educational environments in which reading or writing are combined in particular ways at particular developmental stages. This research would provide both a test of the validity of the model as well as practical information about teaching.

SUMMARY

Various forms of research have supported the theoretical contention that reading and writing rely on analogous mental processes and isomorphic knowledge. However, the total amount of shared variance among a number of reading and writing indicators has never been documented to be more than about .50. Consequently, it is also important to acknowledge the separability of reading and writing. Research has not isolated many of the specific features that make reading and writing unique from one another. Further evidence suggests that, over time, as reading and writing are learned, the nature of their relation changes.

Notably, only limited attention has been directed toward the creation of a developmental model of reading–writing relations or to even a developmental model of writing. Such theoretical work seems necessary to further instructional practice and research and theory in the areas of reading and writing.

In this article, we attempted to devise a very preliminary description of a developmental perspective on the relation of reading and writing. In this model, because of the dearth of prior research on the specific areas of uniqueness between reading and writing, we have focused only on the commonalties or shared cognitive abilities that cut across both reading and writing. Clearly, far more work needs to be done to more completely describe this model and to evaluate its implications with various groups of readers and writers. Still, perhaps by making a start, and by considering the instructional, empirical, and theoretical implications of such a model, some ground is laid for discussion and critique.

REFERENCES

Adams, M. J. (1990). *Beginning to read: Thinking and learning about print.* Cambridge, MA: MIT Press.

Aydelott, S. T. (1998). A study of the reading/writing connection in a university writing program. In E. G. Sturtevant & J. Dugan (Eds.), *Literacy and community* (Twentieth Yearbook of the College Reading Association, pp. 101–114). Carrollton, GA: Beacon.

Beal, C. R. (1996). The role of comprehension monitoring in children's revision. *Educational Psychology Review, 8,* 219–238.

Bear, D. R., Invernizzi, M., Templeton, S., & Johnston, F. (1996). *Words their way.* Englewood Cliffs, NJ: Prentice Hall.

Beaton, A., Guest, J., & Ved, R. (1997). Semantic errors of naming, reading, writing, and drawing following left-hemisphere infarction. *Cognitive Neuropsychology, 14,* 459–478.

Bereiter, C., & Scardamalia, M. (1987). *The psychology of written composition.* Hillsdale, NJ: Lawrence Erlbaum Associates, Inc.

Boget, T., & Marcos, T. (1997). Reading and writing impairments and rehabilitation. In J. Leon-Carrion (Ed.), *Neuropsychological rehabilitation: Fundamentals, innovations and directions* (pp. 333–352). Delray Beach, FL: St. Lucie Press.

Burns, M. S., Griffin, P., & Snow, C. E. (1999). *Starting out right: A guide to promoting children's reading success.* Washington, DC: National Academy Press.

Chall, J. S. (1996). *Stages of reading development.* Fort Worth, TX: Harcourt Brace.

Chan, J. L. (1992). Alexia and agraphia in four Chinese stroke patients with review of the literature: A proposal for a universal mechanism model for reading and writing. *Journal of Neurolinguistics, 7,* 171–185.

Clarke, L. K. (1988). Invented versus traditional spelling in first graders' writings: Effects on learning to spell and read. *Research in the Teaching of English, 22,* 281–309.

Clay, M. M. (1993). *An observation survey of early literacy achievement.* Portsmouth, NH: Heinemann.

Clifford, G. J. (1989). A Sisyphean task: Historical perspectives on writing and reading instruction. In A. H. Dyson (Ed.), *Collaboration through writing and reading* (pp. 25–83). Urbana, IL: National Council of Teachers of English.

Couzijn, M. (1999). Learning to write by observation of writing and reading processes: Effects on learning and transfer. *Learning & Instruction, 9,* 109–142.

Cronnell, B. A. (1970). *Spelling-to-sound correspondences for reading vs. sound-to-spelling correspondences* (Tech. Note 2–70–15). Los Alomitos, CA: Southwest Regional Laboratory.

Ehri, L. (1997). Learning to read and having to spell are one and same, almost. In C. A. Perfetti & L. Rieten (Eds.), *Learning to spell: Research, theory, and practice* (pp. 237–269). Mahwah, NJ: Lawrence Erlbaum Associates, Inc.

Erickson, B., Hubler, M., Bean, T. W., Smith, C. C., & McKenzie, J. V. (1987). Increasing critical reading in junior high classrooms. *Journal of Reading, 30,* 430–439.

Faigley, L., & Witte, S. (1981). Analyzing revision. *College Composition and Communication, 32,* 400–414.

Ferroli, L., & Shanahan, T. (1987). Kindergarten spelling: Explaining its relationship to first-grade reading. In J. E. Readence & R. Scott Baldwin (Eds.), *Research in literacy: Merging perspectives* (Thirty-sixth Yearbook of the National Reading Conference, pp. 93–100). Rochester, NY: National Reading Conference.

Fitzgerald, J. (1989). Enhancing two related thought processes: Revision in writing and critical reading. *The Reading Teacher, 42,* 42–48.

Fitzgerald, J. (1990). Reading and writing as "mind meeting." In T. Shanahan (Ed.), *Reading and writing together: New perspectives for the classroom* (pp. 81–97). Norwood, MA: Christopher-Gordon.

Fitzgerald, J. (1992). *Towards knowledge in writing: Illustrations from revision studies.* New York: Springer-Verlag.

Flower, L. (1994). A cognitive process theory of writing. In R. B. Ruddell & M. R. Ruddell (Eds.), *Theoretical models and processes of reading* (4th ed., pp. 928–950). Newark, DE: International Reading Association.

Frith, U. (1980). Unexpected spelling problems. In U. Frith (Ed.), *Cognitive processes in spelling* (pp. 495–516). London: Academic.

Gentry, J. R., & Gillet, J. W. (1993). *Teaching kids to spell.* Portsmouth, NH: Heinemann.

Gesell, A. L. (1925). *Infancy and human growth.* New York: Macmillan.

Kaestle, C. F. (1985). The history of literacy and the history of readers. *Review of Research in Education, 12,* 11–53.

Kellogg, R. (1994). *The psychology of writing.* New York: Oxford University Press.

King, M. L., & Rentel, V. (1979). Toward a theory of early writing development. *Research in the Teaching of English, 13,* 243–253.

Klare, G. R. (1974–1975). Assessing readability. *Reading Research Quarterly, 10,* 62–102.

Langer, J. A. (1986). *Children reading and writing: Structures and strategies.* Norwood, NJ: Ablex.

Lenski, S. D. (1998). Strategic knowledge when reading in order to write. *Reading Psychology, 19,* 287–315.

Loban, W. (1976). *Language development.* Urbana, IL: National Council of Teachers of English.

Nelson, N., & Calfee, R. C. (1998a). The reading–writing connection. In N. Nelson & R. C. Calfee (Eds.), *Ninety-seventh Yearbook of the National Society for the Study of Education* (Part II, pp. 1–52). Chicago: National Society for the Study of Education.

Nelson, N., & Calfee, R. C. (1998b). The reading–writing connection viewed historically. In N. Nelson & R. C. Calfee (Eds.), *Ninety-seventh Yearbook of the National Society for the Study of Education* (Part II, pp. 1–52). Chicago: National Society for the Study of Education.

New Standards Primary Literacy Standards Committee. (1999). *Reading & writing grade by grade.* Washington, DC: National Center on Education and the Economy.

Niemi, P., Poskiparta, E., Vaurus, M., & Maeki, H. (1998). Reading and writing difficulties do not always occur as the researcher expects. *Scandinavian Journal of Psychology, 39,* 159–161.

Nystrand, M. (1989). A social-interactive model of writing. *Written Communication, 6,* 66–85.

Pascarella, E. T., Edison, M. I., Nora, A., Hagedorn, L. S., & Terenzini, P. T. (1998). Does work inhibit cognitive development during college? *Educational Evaluation & Policy Analysis, 20,* 75–93.

Perin, D. (1998). Assessing the reading–writing relation in adult literacy students. *Reading Psychology, 19,* 141–183.

Perry, W. (1970). *Forms of intellectual and ethical development in the college years: A scheme.* New York: Holt, Rinehart & Winston.

Reuter, Y. (1993). *Les interactions lecture-écriture* [The integration of reading–writing]. New York/Paris: Peter Lang.

Santa, C. M., & Hoien, T. (1999). An assessment of Early Steps: A program for early intervention of reading problems. *Reading Research Quarterly, 34,* 54–79.

Schwartz, R. M. (1997). Self-monitoring in beginning reading. *The Reading Teacher, 51,* 40–48.

Shanahan, T. (1984). Nature of the reading–writing relation: An exploratory multivariate analysis. *Journal of Educational Psychology, 76,* 466–477.

Shanahan, T. (1988). The reading–writing relationship: Seven instructional principles. *The Reading Teacher, 41,* 636–647.

Shanahan, T., & Lomax, R. G. (1986). An analysis and comparison of theoretical models of the reading–writing relationship. *Journal of Educational Psychology, 78,* 116–123.

Shanahan, T., & Lomax, R. G. (1988). A developmental comparison of three theoretical models of the reading–writing relationship. *Research in the Teaching of English, 22,* 196–212.

Shanahan, T., & Tierney, R. J. (1990). Reading–writing relationships: Three perspectives. In J. Zutell & S. McCormick (Eds.), *Literacy theory and research: Analyses from multiple paradigms* (Thirty-ninth Yearbook of the National Reading Conference, pp. 13–34). Chicago: National Reading Conference.

Shell, D. F., Colvin, C., & Bruning, R. H. (1995). Self-efficacy, attribution, and outcome expectancy mechanisms in reading and writing achievement: Grade-level and achievement-level differences. *Journal of Educational Psychology, 87*, 368–398.

Slotte, C., & Lanka, K. (1999). Review of process effects of spontaneous note-taking on text comprehension. *Contemporary Educational Psychology, 24*, 1–20.

Stotsky, S. (1983). Research on reading/writing relationships: A synthesis and suggested directions. *Language Arts, 60*, 627–643.

Straw, S. B., & Schreiner, R. (1982). The effect of sentence manipulation on subsequent measures of reading and listening. *Reading Research Quarterly, 17*, 335–352.

Teale, W. H., & Sulzby, E. (Eds.). (1986). *Emergent literacy: Writing and reading*. Norwood, NJ: Ablex.

Tierney, R. J. (1983, December). *Analyzing composing behavior: Planning, aligning, revising*. Paper presented at the 33rd annual National Reading Conference, Austin, TX.

Tierney, R. J., & Pearson, P. D. (1983). Toward a composing model of reading. *Language Arts, 60*, 568–580.

Tierney, R. J., & Shanahan, T. (1991). Research on the reading–writing relationship: Interactions, transactions, and outcomes. In R. Barr, M. L. Kamil, P. Mosenthal, & P. D. Pearson (Eds.), *The handbook of reading research* (Vol. 2, pp. 246–280). New York: Longman.

Tierney, R. J., Soter, A., O'Flahavan, J. F., & McGinley, W. (1989). The effects of reading and writing upon thinking critically. *Reading Research Quarterly, 24*, 134–173.

Tunmer, W. E., & Nesdale, A. R. (1985). Phonemic segmentation skill and beginning reading. *Journal of Educational Psychology, 77*, 417–427.

Tymms, P. (1999). Baseline assessment, value-added and the prediction of reading. *Journal of Research in Reading, 22*, 27–36.

Wharton-McDonald, R., Pressley, M., & Hampton, J. M. (1998). Literary instruction in nine first-grade classrooms: Teacher characteristics and student achievement. *Elementary School Journal, 99*, 101–128.

Wood, F., Bruner, J. S., & Ross, G. (1976). The role of tutoring in problem solving. *Journal of Child Psychiatry, 17*, 89–100.

EDUCATIONAL PSYCHOLOGIST, *35*(1), 51–62

Society's Child: Social Context and Writing Development

Katherine Schultz

Department of Educational Leadership
University of Pennsylvania

Bob Fecho

Department of Reading Education
University of Georgia

This article draws from discussions that have been taking place over the last 20 years concerning the interplay of social contextual research and theory and knowledge about writing development. Beginning with a survey of these academic discussions and then detailing what this theory suggests through an examination of the academic literature and classroom examples, the article suggests that writing development is (a) reflective of social historical contexts, (b) variable across local contexts, (c) reflective of classroom curriculum and pedagogy, (d) shaped by social interactions, (e) tied to social identities, and (f) conceptualized as a nonlinear process. It then argues that a social contextual stance on writing development shifts perspective not away from the individual writer and the individual product, but toward seeing that writer and text in multiple contexts that complicate our understanding of writing process.

In this article, we draw from discussions that have been taking place over the last 20 years about the interplay of social contextual research and theory and knowledge about writing development. These discussions, at various times, have divided, perplexed, and even united the composition community (Nystrand, Greene, & Wiemelt, 1993). For example, consideration of social contextual issues has led to arguments that the field of composition studies has become too political (Hairston, 1992), too politically naïve (Villanueva, 1997), and too politically narrow (Rose, 1985). The growing prominence of anthropological research that included ethnographic studies of writing and literacy (e.g., Heath, 1983; Street, 1984) led to this new field of research that had and continues to have implications for practice and theory.

Our purpose is to consider what it means to take such a perspective in writing research and what happens—to pedagogy, to students' concepts of themselves as writers, to writing development, in particular—when social contextual issues are given substantive consideration as writing is theorized and taught (for discussions, see Barton, 1991; Cooper & Holzman, 1989; Dyson & Freedman, 1991; Nystrand et al., 1993). By first surveying the landscape of these academic discussions and then detailing what this theory suggests through an examination of the academic literature and classroom examples, we illustrate what the academic community has come to know, what seems to be the prevailing thought, and what questions these perspectives raise for future considerations of writing development.

However, before we can begin this discussion, we need to acknowledge a crossing of paradigms and what that means for the reader. To consider a social contextual perspective, one has to understand something of the worldview and vocabulary that sustain such a lens. Affected greatly by both poststructural and postmodern thinking, educators taking a social contextual view of writing development perceive the world as socially constructed, where knowledge is in flux and issues are complicated by deep structures of multiply-perceived meaning. Therefore, causal relations are difficult to ascertain due to the multiplicity of variables that could either by themselves or in combination affect the outcome. What we come to know and understand about a subject is contextualized in the time, place, and circumstances within which the knowing was constructed. As a result, social contextual research is largely descriptive and interpretive, employing primarily anthropologic traditions of ethnographic study. Given these considerations, a social contextual perspective on writing development, much like the literature it draws on, will be more descriptive in nature.

Requests for reprints should be sent to Katherine Schultz, University of Pennsylvania, Graduate School of Education, 3700 Walnut Street, Philadelphia, PA 19104. E-mail: kathys@gse.upenn.edu

SURVEYING THE LANDSCAPE

We begin our discussion of writing research in the 1970s, when literacy researchers from various paradigms turned from a study of texts to an examination of writing processes or individuals composing. Beginning with the groundbreaking work of Emig (1971), researchers looked at writing development in ways that focused on individuals and defined writing less as a product and more as a collection of processes, including, among other factors, problem solving, attention to audience, and notions of recursivity (see Cooper & Odell, 1978; Flower & Hayes, 1981; Tate, 1976). Much of this newer work was written in response to early cognitive models of writing. However, as Flower (1989) admitted "Early work in cognition … focused on the individual" (p. 283) and failed to develop a theory to explain how the social context might shape composing and what institutionalized forms of writing might mean to the writer. She goes on to point out that early cognitive research was not blind to issues of social theory—a conception of audience and task environment were usually taken into account in process models—but these models rarely went further to imagine the impact of social theory for the examination of composing processes. Cognitive researchers were grappling with the notion of social context and often added it as a static factor in their models of writing.

In response to this interest in understanding writing in social contexts, literacy researchers familiar with anthropological theories and methods studied literacy in and out of school contexts (e.g., Barton, 1991; Heath, 1983; Street, 1984). In addition, a set of initiatives based on practice—teaching basic writing at the university, conducting teacher research, developing critical inquiry pedagogy, and responding to cultures of students in the classroom—combined to push educators beyond a single focus on the individual learner to a broader lens that considered that learner's many contexts for meaning making. Although space does not permit us to discuss the impact of each of these movements, it is important to understand that, like the role multiple contexts play for the individual writer, social contextual aspects of education were also under consideration in many arenas. Perhaps most significant for our purposes here is that each was in some way a response to social issues that were in the forefront of daily, political, and educational life and also had clear ties to uses and conceptions of literacy. Therefore, educators were raising questions into which only investigations into social theories of literacy could adequately provide insight.

To illustrate this point, we briefly discuss the manner in which these dynamics played out in relation to basic writing classes at the university level. These classes were a response to open admissions policies adopted widely by universities in the late 1960s. In that decade, college classrooms suddenly became more than the purview of privileged white students, but were places where students from the full spectrum of cultures represented in the United States were granted access to higher education. This situation raised questions about the teaching of writing and writing development, because many students whose writing differed markedly from the standard edited English so valued by the academy were enrolled in university classes. Early responses to this challenge were deeply embedded in cognitive theory (e.g., Lunsford, 1979); however, the work of Mina Shaughnessy (1976, 1977) began to point toward social issues as they related to basic writers. She, along with others, raised the key question of whether these students should adopt the values of the academy or whether the academy needed to reconsider its conventions of writing. Charting her own progress from a guardian of the ivory towers to a teacher who was willing to "become a student of new disciplines and of [her] students themselves in order to perceive both their difficulties and their incipient excellence" (1976, p. 239), she urged teachers to learn about their students from the students themselves and for both students and teachers to see divergence from standard edited English as a window into the minds of the students (Shaughnessy, 1977).

Building on the work of Shaughnessy (1977) and their own classroom-based research, researchers at the Center for the Study of Writing at Berkeley and Carnegie Mellon were leaders in defining a sociocognitive perspective on literacy (Freedman, Dyson, Flower, & Chafe, 1987). Later, this sociocognitive lens became redefined as a sociocultural and historical perspective to account for the importance of the social, cultural, and historical contexts of literacy practices and development (Brodkey, 1987; Dyson & Freedman, 1991; Freedman, Flower, Hull, & Hayes, 1995; Hull & Rose, 1989, 1990; Rose, 1985, 1988).

The intent here is not to construct a social history of the 1970s and 1980s. Instead, the purpose is to inject an awareness that educational initiatives were developing in the emerging field of composition study that urged interrogation of the significant yet particular contribution that cognitive models were making to our understanding of the writing process. Essentially, educators involved in these social contextual movements were asking the same question: If humans are social beings who exist in complexly intermeshed cultural structures, to what extent is our education constructed by those structures and to what extent does education socially construct our images of various cultures? For example, how does the culture of school and the home culture of basic writers collide in ways that derail the efforts of those writers in academic settings? If learning, as Freire (1970) suggested, is dialogic in nature, what does that look like in the writing classroom? If race, gender, and other cultural identities matter in the social structure, what does that mean for expressing one's identity through writing?

For many, the answers to these questions, or at least a direction for seeking greater understanding, could be found in the works of Vygotsky (e.g., 1934/1962, 1978) and Bakhtin (e.g., 1981, 1986). Born within a year of each other and working at approximately the same time period in Marxist Russia, both theorists, as Schuster (1997) noted, focused their work in different areas but came to "celebrate language as the means through which human beings understand the world and themselves" (p. 472). Additionally, the work of both scholars underwent suppression and rediscovery, with the work of Vygotsky coming to light to the Western world in the early 1960s and that of Bakhtin 20 years later. Despite these congruencies, there is little evidence to suggest that the two scholars were influenced by each other. As Schuster explained, Bakhtin may have read some early work by Vygotsky but, despite numerous citations of other scholarship, never cited him. However, Vygotsky's (1934/1962) theories of the ways thought and language connect and Bakhtin's (1981) belief in the dialogic nature of speech entered the academic imagination simultaneously as educators who had a stake in composition theory asked about the role of social context as it related to writing development.

Although there is evidence of Vygotsky's theories being used to support cognitive models of composing (see D'Angelo, 1978; Emig, 1977), it was not until publication of *Mind and Society* in 1978 that the greater social contextual relevance of his work and its importance to composition theory took hold. As suggested by Cazden (1996), those interested in writing theory tend to use Vygotsky selectively to make various arguments. Frequently, however, educators who take social contextual views of writing development identify Vygotsky's (1934/1962, 1978) discussion of inner speech and his concept of scaffolded learning embodied in his concept of the zone of proximal development (ZPD) as a useful theoretic frame. In terms of inner speech, Vygotsky (1934/1962) described the relation between language and thought and particularly emphasized the deep structure of inner speech where "a single word is so saturated with sense that many words would be required to explain it in external speech" (p. 148). Because of this saturation, Vygotsky suggested that to understand what someone is saying, we need to understand what she or he is thinking and even the motivation behind the thought. In a Vygotskian cosmos, therefore, language appears to be embedded in the context of the utterance. The ZPD (Vygotsky, 1978) is a place of shifting circumstances wherein the learners gradually take on more responsibility for their own learning through guided or scaffolded instruction from a more experienced other. From this, learning can be construed as collaborative and dependent on interaction. It is inherently social.

Although Vygotsky's (1934/1962, 1978) research and writing suggests a social contextual perspective for describing writing development, the connections are more implied than direct. We agree with Cazden (1996) when she argued that the work of Bakhtin (1981) provides a more explicit discussion of the role of social contextual theory in understanding the ways we write. We also agree that taking the theories of Vygotsky in tandem with those of Bakhtin does much to maximize the work of both theorists. Vygotsky's (1934/1962) sense of saturation is markedly akin to Bakhtin's (1981) belief that language comes to us "populated—over-populated—with the intentions of others" (p. 294) and

"tast[ing] of the context and contexts in which it has lived its socially charged life" (p. 293). In a Bakhtinian classroom, the word is embedded in a context of individual and societal importance. Language becomes one's own only when expropriated from others. The language of place, of culture, of career, to name just a few social discourses, intermingles within writers, and the resulting transactions are part of the dialogic nature of the composing process. Conceptualized as dynamic, discourse is pictured as being in a constant state of becoming as individuals interact with each other's language and alternately impart and take on that which flows through this dialogic tide.

We are not making a causal argument here. It is not our intent that the publication of translations of Bakhtin (1981, 1986) and Vygotsky's (1934/1962, 1978) work singularly led to a questioning of society's impact on learning. As we have noted, many educational initiatives were underway that were raising these questions. Nor did an interest by U.S. educators in social contextual aspects of learning lead Vygotsky and Bakhtin to consider these concerns. We know that most of this work was conducted in the early third of this century. Instead, our argument is that there is a transactional relation. As the world shifted into the last decades of the 20th century, many educators sensed that who we are as individuals and how we either identify or dis-identify with the various cultures of our lives had an impact on our ability to learn. In particular, the ways these issues connect to writing became important because of the paradigm shift initiated by cognitive theorists seeing writing not only as a product, but also as a recursive and complex process. It was the combination of these social movements and the availability and discussion of this research that spurred the research directions we track in the following section.

CONSIDERING NOTIONS OF WRITING DEVELOPMENT

We cannot begin a discussion of writing development without some unpacking of the term itself. To this end, we open with a description of Roderick, an African American writer from a fourth-grade class at an urban public school (summarized from Schultz, 1997).

At the beginning of his fourth-grade year, Roderick's sentences were short, his pictures were packed with meaning. An accomplished artist, Roderick's drawings not only contained the story line, they entertained and educated his peers who regularly checked in with him to "read" his new story. While they appreciated his skill and the sophisticated sense of humor evident in the drawings, Roderick's teachers felt obligated to prepare him for the demands of middle school. They prompted him to write every day, at times keeping him in from recess to insure that he had a few sentences on his page.

Reluctantly, and at his own pace, Roderick found reasons to write and by the end of the year had crafted elaborate and relatively long, contemporary urban versions of Greek hero tales.

Early writing researchers who looked at writing in naturalistic settings described growth or development in writing in terms of stages based on a sequence of skills appropriate for all students that included the mastery of conventions such as spelling, discourse structures, and revision (e.g., King & Rentel, 1979). Viewed from this paradigm, Roderick might be described as proceeding along an orderly path of writing development, moving from drawing to story writing, and evidence for his growth would be found in a close textual analysis of his written products.

In a classic study, Moffett (1968) expanded the notion of writing development in his exploration of genres through a description of the situatedness of learning to write and the individual paths of writers. Likewise, Britton, Burgess, Martin, McLeod, and Rosen (1975) defined writing development as a cognitive activity that involved poetic and transactional language and the interaction of social conditions and individual minds. As precursors to current, more complex understandings of writing development, these definitions focus on single aspects of individual growth and point toward a sociocognitive perspective at the same time that they fail to adequately capture the full complexity of that stance.

A contribution of social contextual research is to complicate our understanding of an individual's growth as a writer and to not only see it as layered but to embrace its intricate nature. This perspective urges us to pay attention to social contextual dimensions along with the individual's actions and texts. These dimensions include the historical, cultural, and social identities the individual brings to writing, the social world in which the writing occurs, the peer and teacher interactions that surround the writing, and the classroom organization, including the curriculum and pedagogical decisions made by the teacher and school. Researchers who take a social contextual perspective look at multiple and overlapping dimensions of writing that are intertwined in unpredictable ways. Building on work with adult learners, Lytle (1991) articulated a conceptual framework for literacy development that accounted for adults' beliefs, practices, language processes, and plans (see also Lytle & Schultz, 1990). In doing so, Lytle urged us to rethink our assumptions about development, literacy, and learning for adults, and she raised questions critical to our examination of writing development across the life span.

A social contextual description of Roderick's growth as a writer might focus on his use of writing as a social tool (Vygotsky, 1934/1962, 1978) and would emphasize the ways in which he encountered and used writing through a range of contexts, in different social relationships, to produce a variety of written products. Such a description would delineate the ways in which he took up the available discourses in his class-

room and detail how he wrote to, for, and with his peers and teachers to join the classroom community. Roderick's growth would be pictured as multidimensional, tied to the historical time, the local context, and the proclivities he brought to each literacy event (Schultz, 1997). As Dyson (1990) explained, "The child's emerging control of any symbol system is simultaneously the child's increasingly active participation in a cultural dialogue" (p. 10). Taking a social contextual view of writing development, Dyson asserts that the development of written language involves a complicated relation between the representation of symbols and the negotiation of social worlds. According to Dyson, writing development occurs in a range of contexts that include a variety of functions and forms.

Bringing a sociolinguistic view to this discussion, Hicks (1996) gave us parameters for documenting writing development that she termed "learning." She described in detail the ways in which learning occurs as students navigate the social world of the classroom and both internalize and reconstruct the discourses constitutive of that environment. She conceptualized learning as a "boundary phenomenon," as transactional rather than the property of either the student or the culture. Thus, the documentation of writing development includes an examination of oral and written texts along with the study of the individual's participation in the social and discursive activity that surrounds the writing. As Hicks explained:

> In short, what I am suggesting as a methodology for examining the emergent qualities of social meaning construction and also the boundary between individual and social meanings are multiple layers of interpretive analysis. If the theoretical goal is one of articulating the dialectic between what is "inside" the child and what is "out there" in culture, then neither analyses of textual products nor inferential studies of cognitive process alone are sufficient. (p. 112)

Development, according to Hicks, can thus be viewed in this larger sociocultural context and must take into account individual actions, textual constructions, and social phenomenon.

Dyson (1990) further complicated this view by arguing that a social contextual perspective of writing development can be found not merely by looking at individuals or texts, but by looking at individuals—including their social identities, histories, interests, purposes, and goals—in relation to their peers, teachers, and audiences. In a recent article, Dyson (1999) described her research that looks at the ways that children use cultural artifacts to enter into school literacy. She asked: "What does written language development look like—how does one write a narrative of child change—if learning is conceived of as a process of text appropriation and recontextualization, rather than pure invention or apprenticeship?" (p. 374). Dyson described development as occurring when students have agency and she urged teachers to see the possibilities in children's culture to mediate between their worlds and the world of school.

From studies such as these, we suggest that writing development can be conceptualized as a transaction among individual learners, their many contexts, and the sign and symbol system. The following section describes in more specific detail what this means for understanding students' growth as writers.

A SOCIAL CONTEXTUAL PERSPECTIVE ON WRITING DEVELOPMENT

Our analysis of recent research that takes a social contextual view on writing and writing development suggests that writing development is (a) reflective of social historical contexts, (b) variable across local contexts, (c) reflective of classroom curriculum and pedagogy, (d) shaped by social interactions, (e) tied to social identities, and (f) conceptualized as a nonlinear process. Our discussion of each of these propositions includes a general discussion of relevant literature and one or two illustrative studies. For clarity, we present each of these propositions as if it were a discrete category or dimension. In practice, there is much overlap among these ideas.

Writing Development Reflects Social Historical Contexts

Writing development both reflects and contributes to the social historical and political context and institutional relations in which it occurs. A focus on the broader contexts surrounding writers and writing leads to an examination of power, equity, and access. For instance, it leads us to examine what writing and which writers are included and which are excluded from consideration in a study of writing and writing development. Similarly, it raises questions about what writing and which writers are deemed acceptable—and teachable and thus invited into university settings—and who is kept out of the academy. For instance, Ivanic (1998) illustrated the ways students position themselves differently in academic communities according to their choices of discursive practices. She connected these decisions to their personal histories of opportunities, constraints, and allegiances. Thus, power and experience contribute to an individual's growth as a writer by not only influencing what individuals write, but also who is allowed to write, for whom, in what contexts, and under which constraints.

Delpit (1995) described this transactional relation between writing and access. She asserted that even as people learn conventional ways to write—what she terms *the power code*—they are acting on and transforming it. Thus, learning to write for a particular context, including the academy, entails learning the rules but also may involve the transformation of those conventions. A social contextual

perspective on writing development helps us to understand the ways in which people write with and against culture and how these choices shape their growth as writers. When people refuse to participate in academic discourses, their actions can be framed as resistance or as an active stance against a dominant ideology (Giroux, 1983). This perspective reframes failure as sometimes being an act of choice and refocuses our ways of looking at and understanding writing and writing development.

Making a broader claim, Cazden (1996) pointed out that an important legacy of Vygotsky (1934/1962, 1978) is that language is rarely studied in isolation but in relation to social, historical, cultural, and political processes. Using Street's (1984, 1995) description of the ideological nature of literacy, Clark and Ivanic (1997) detailed the ways in which the social practices of writing are shaped by power (see also Fairclough, 1989). This includes who is allowed access to particular kinds of writing and writing practices (Bizzell, 1989). Such a view of writing shifts our understanding away from the depiction of writing as a technical or even a personal activity to one that is shaped by both local and larger cultural, historical, and ideological forces. Writing frames who we are at the same time that our writing reflects the historical moment in which we reside, threaded by social, political, and cultural dimensions.

In a teacher researcher study, Goldblatt (1995) explicitly used a social theory of composition to examine the process of three struggling urban high school students as they attempted to become "authors," a term he employs to reflect a writer in a social context of power and institutional relations. He was particularly interested in the ways in which writing both challenged and extended cultural institutions and the ways in which institutions shaped the authority of individuals. Using DuBois's (1903/1961) term "double consciousness," Goldblatt described how marginalized students must be fluent in at least two discourses and analyzed the ways a disjuncture between public and private selves can be a hindrance to writing. He concluded that we should build composition theory and writing pedagogy in such a way that we pay attention to how cultural conditions affect the disenfranchised writers who sit on the edge of the community.

Writing Development Varies Across Local Contexts

The contexts of writing are shaped by the group norms of differently situated writing communities. A social perspective on writing suggests that writing does not only occur in school or the workplace, at a desk or on the word processor, but that, for most of us, writing begins when we wake up in the morning and continues until we put down our writing instruments at the end of the day (Barton, 1991). In addition, writing that occurs at home or in the workplace may differ from that which takes place in the classroom, and thus writing development can be said to occur across multiple contexts that are shaped by the group norms of differentially situated writing communities. These contexts include the genres, the purposes for writing, and the audiences—both real and imagined—for the text. In addition, the contexts account for the particular task and the rhetorical conventions that shape the task. Thus, a particular text, and the writer's composition of that text, must be understood in light of the writer's own understanding of the task in concert with conventional knowledge and those held by the teachers or persons assigning the writing task itself. One way to examine the significance of the local context of writing is to consider writing practices outside of a traditional school setting.

Ethnographers of communication (cf. Gumperz, 1981; Heath, 1983; Hymes, 1972) looked outside of classrooms to document reading, writing, and language use as social practices. In a series of studies in Philadelphia, Fiering (1981) and Gilmore (1983), among others, studied unofficial writing and literacy activities in urban schools and documented the ways in which students were skillful in out-of-school contexts at the same time they were viewed as poor writers in school. More recently, Heath and McLaughlin (1993) wrote about the literacy practices of students in after-school contexts and suggested the need to look outside of schools and classrooms for evidence of students' talents and abilities and their growth in writing. Subsequently, Hull and Schultz (1998) argued for using this understanding of writing in out-of-school contexts as a means for informing literacy practices inside of schools. Rather than giving up on schools as sites for learning, they argue that lessons learned from the careful study of writing outside of school can be used to inform writing pedagogy and curriculum inside of schools. This argument is predicated on the importance of understanding in detail the ways in which local contexts shape writing practices and leads to the proposition that writing and writing development must be viewed in the local contexts of particular communities.

A study of the literacy practices of workers in a reorganized circuit board assembly plant in the Silicon Valley (Gee, Hull, & Lankshear, 1996; Hull, Jury, Ziv, & Katz, 1996) illustrated the multiple functions and uses of writing across contexts. At this circuit board assembly plant, a workforce of recent immigrants and people of color born in this country work in a large and successful factory organized into teams to assemble circuit boards. They participate in team competitions in which front-line workers use overheads, pareto charts, and fishbone diagrams to illustrate the problems their self-directed work teams have solved in the previous month (Hull et al., 1996). To describe how these workers use literacy and thus how their writing develops over time, the local contexts surrounding the writing must be understood, including the tasks and power relations within those tasks.

It is critical to not only look at the texts produced by the teams of workers—the actual charts and diagrams—but also the social conditions under which they were produced and used as the literacy events. An understanding of these workers as writers is necessarily shaped by the interactions that preceded and follow the composition of the texts. It also depends on the perceived and real purposes of the texts themselves, the social construction of the team meeting as a particular kind of event at this historical moment and in this factory that is inventing a version of restructuring. For instance, the competitive nature of the event and the workers' cultural understandings and relation to competition shape their participation in the event and thus the way in which they produced the document. In addition, the local understanding of competition and collaboration, as well as the hierarchical positions of the workers both at the factory and in the larger community, shaped individuals' participation in the event. The use of the texts in the meeting itself is connected to both the texts themselves and the workers' growth as writers as they produce new texts for subsequent meetings. Thus, an understanding of both the practices of writing and writing development is intimately connected to local circumstances and will change as these contexts change.

Writing Development Reflects Classroom Curriculum and Pedagogy

Writing development is shaped by the curricular and pedagogical decisions made by teachers often in conjunction with students. Classroom cultures and practices produce the environment for writing growth; writing growth cannot be understood apart from the local culture of the classroom. In her study of a writing exchange set up between teachers in urban schools located in the United States and England, Freedman (1994a) detailed the ways in which writing pedagogy and curriculum at the classroom level are shaped by national policies and local understandings of practice. This study, designed to compare learning to write in the two countries, illustrated how different educational policies and institutional structures affect students' writing and their growth as writers. Although the focus of the study was on the exchanges between paired young adolescents in eight classes, Freedman also detailed the nature of interactions between and among teachers and students in each classroom. This close analysis of writing in two countries at the national, as well as the classroom and individual, level emphasizes the ways in which schools are institutions shaped by national policies. Broadly speaking, British teachers negotiated their curriculum with students, giving them choice and flexibility while insuring that each student mastered a variety of genres. They placed greater emphasis than their U.S. counterparts on knowing their students, although their individualization was not at the expense of the community. For their part, the U.S. teachers enacted a range of curricula and pedagogical choices, often following curricular models that led them to focus more on practice than on students. These varied "social spaces" created different conditions for students' growth as writers and students' writing varied along numerous dimensions.

Lensmire (1993, 1994a, 1994b) described the impact of pedagogical and curriculum choices in his research that illustrated how peer interaction shaped the running of a writing workshop in a third-grade public-school classroom. A university-based researcher who spent a year as a writing teacher, Lensmire (1994a) demonstrated the ways in which the peer culture was stratified by hierarchies of power and status, which influenced the production of writing in the context of the writing workshop. Lensmire used the theoretical perspectives of Bakhtin (1981, 1986), Freire (1970, 1985), and others in a critical examination of his own practice that problematizes the writing workshop approach advocated by Atwell (1987), Calkins (1986, 1991), and Graves (1983). Challenging the romantic portrayals of both children as innocent writers and the writing workshop itself as an idealized community, he suggested that these idealized notions tend to focus on writing apart from its social context. He illustrated the complexity of this theory and pedagogy by drawing on the work of Bakhtin (e.g., 1981) to describe the writing workshop in his classroom:

> The dialogically agitated environment of our writing workshop was a struggle over identity, participation, meaning and values. In their talk and texts, children took up conflicting positions on questions of who should tell whose stories, who should speak and be listened to, whose interpretations were valid, how it is we should treat one another. (p. 139)

He concluded that it is not enough to follow the lead of the children as writing workshop enthusiasts advocate. That idealized perspective does not account for the micropolitics, local meanings, traditions, and values, and, in short, occasional unkindness of real children in real contexts. He argued for a reconceptualization of teachers' roles in the writing classroom and suggested that teachers must not only take a leadership role so that their classroom reflects their own beliefs and values, but also that teachers actively take a critical stance on writing and the actions of writers. In essence, he suggested that educators pay attention to the community of writers that we create.

Writing Development Is Shaped by Social Interaction

A social contextual view of writing development makes social interaction a prominent feature in an account of growth in writing. In recognition of the value of teamwork, teachers have recently introduced cooperative learning activities in which students work together to produce a single product. (See Cohen, 1986; Johnson & Johnson, 1987; Slavin, 1991; for discussions of collaboration in writing, see Daiute & Dalton, 1988, 1992; DiPardo & Freedman, 1988; Freedman, 1987, 1994b; Kalman, 1996; Lunsford & Ede, 1990; Schultz, 1994, 1997.) Along similar lines, Ladson-Billings (1994) stressed the importance of cooperative learning and community building in her argument for "culturally relevant" teaching (see also Foster, 1992, and Robinson & Ward, 1991). These two modes of teaching and learning—the privileging of individual work and the promotion of collective work—are frequently posed as polar opposites. Alternatively, however, they can be incorporated into a single vision of collaboration that includes both working together and working alone (Schultz, 1997).

In an interpretive study of the social nature of writing in an urban public third- and fourth-grade classroom, one of us (Schultz, 1994, 1997) detailed the multiple meanings of collaboration between and among students and teachers in a writing classroom. In this classroom, collaboration among students included the following arrangements: Students wrote alone and shared their work with others; they wrote in pairs or small consistent groups termed "networks"; and they worked together to author a single text. Teachers used writing to forge collaborative relationships with students—relationships often rife with struggle and conflict—to encourage students' growth or development as writers. Schultz concluded that whether students wrote alone or in the company of others, traces of the voices of their classmates were combined with their own as they struggled to create their own identities as writers. Thus, collaboration suggests a range of practices, including writing with, and also for, others along with an interrelationship of peers and teachers that must be accounted for in a description of an individual's development as a writer. Finally, collaboration is seen as a strategy for reconceptualizing relationships among students and between students and their teachers and implies possibilities for all participants to co-construct curriculum.

Roderick, the student described at the beginning of this section, exemplifies this dynamic and complex view of collaboration. He was a writer who resisted working directly with his classmates and insisted on the importance of original ideas—actions that implied writing by himself. Yet, although he wrote by himself, Roderick always wrote for others and thus his collaboration could be said to include his teachers and peers as his audience. A description of his growth as a writer must take into account the intricate and multiple relationships he formed in the classroom.

Dyson (e.g., 1993, 1995) wrote extensively about the ways in which social interaction among peers shapes children's growth as writers. Recently, her work centered on the role of popular culture—in particular, superheroes—in the writing and social worlds of school (Dyson, 1997). Dyson claimed that, as composers, students sit at the nexus of social and ideological worlds shaped by the complexity of our contemporary times. They negotiate meaning using the words, discourses, or signs that are available to them. Dyson documented the interaction between children's own writing processes and their participation in their multiethnic classroom community or social world. This work illustrates the ways in which children's stories are shaped by their desire to join their social community and their need to find their own place in a diverse world. In this classroom, writing became a way of extending and acting out social play. She concluded that sociocultural diversity is a significant and rich resource for both teachers and the children in the classroom. In contrast to writing workshop advocates from the 1970s and 1980s (e.g., Graves, 1983), Dyson (1997) described a "pedagogy of responsibility" (p. 180)—a way of teaching that links the individual and his or her composing to the larger community. Thus, an individual doesn't "own" the meaning of his or her work; rather it is explicitly a negotiated meaning set in the classroom or large social context. This has interesting implications for understanding writing development not only as an individual phenomenon but also as an activity tied closely to the social and ideological dimensions of literacy learning in the classroom.

Writing Development Is Tied to Social Identities

Writing reflects who we are at the same time that it shapes our identity. A framework with which to understand writing that includes an examination of the social and historical identities of a writer leads to the following questions: Who is the writer; what are the circumstances under which the writer is learning to write; and in what directions is the writer going?

Gee (1989, 1996) defined *primary Discourses* as the ways of being, talking, doing, and valuing that children acquire through enculturation in intimate contexts at home and in their communities. *Secondary Discourses* are associated with schools, institutions, and workplaces and, as compared to primary Discourses, are learned rather than acquired. Using a capital D to indicate this larger, more global view of discourses as identity toolkits rather than textual forms, Gee emphasized that we never completely learn these secondary Discourses. He asserted that each of us is a member of many discourse communities, adding that each Discourse represents one of our identities. His research suggests that if language is shaped by ideology and can not be analyzed apart from it, then writing development, too, must be viewed as tied intimately to social identities.

One of us (Fecho, 1998, 2000) described and analyzed the critical inquiry about language and learning that he engaged in with his students as a teacher researcher. He raised questions about how language choices are tied to identity and described students' reluctance to use standard English and their articulation of the ways it changed how they perceived themselves and how others saw them. In his urban high school classroom, African and Caribbean American working-class students crossed cultural boundaries as they argued and theorized about language and power and the ways in which their lives were shaped by how they chose to write and speak. Fecho (1998, 2000) used students' speech and writing to complicate notions of writing pedagogy and development,

adding multiple and, at times, conflicting perspectives that were firmly rooted in students' social identities to the discussions of standard English. He illustrated how students learned—both as individuals and as members of a classroom community—the power of using language to inquire, theorize, and take a stance on issues intimately related to their lives. His research suggested that the social identities of the students had an impact on their learning and writing development. In asking students to research their own uses of language rather than imposing a rule of using standard English in their writing and speech, Fecho (1998, 2000) shifted the power dynamics in his classroom, thus opening up possibilities for learning and growth.

Writing Development Is a Nonlinear Process

Writing growth can be said to occur on a nonlinear path. Such a conception allows us to track students' progress and account for its complexity without an overreliance on a normative model of development. It also allows for individual variation and a more complex understanding of development. Because individuals have different stylistic and cultural preferences for making sense and expressing meaning (Bussis, Chittenden, Amarel, & Klausner, 1985; Carini, 1987), there is no single template for learning to write. In their study of the literacy knowledge children acquire before they attend school, Harste, Woodward, and Burke (1984) found that children, even those living in what were thought to be impoverished circumstances, had accumulated vast resources prior to school. They reminded us that, when we focus on texts as products and signs of development, we see some types of growth and opportunities for learning but fail to see others. They wrote: "Researchers studying what young children know about print have found children in a state of 'cognitive confusion.' After many years of work in this area, however, we have yet to find a child who is cognitively confused" (p. 32). In other words, when researchers and educators abandon the linear measurement of students' growth as writers, they see the individual ways students make sense of the world and express their sense-making through print.

Students bring varied resources—for example, knowledge of text structures, orthography, grammar, genres—and diverse modes of interaction with people and symbolic media to the task of writing (Dyson, 1987). In addition, when students attempt a more difficult task (e.g., a new genre), writers may appear to "go backwards" in terms of their use of mechanics or other writing conventions. If viewed within a sequential and uniform conception of writing development—in other words, with the assumption that all children follow a single trajectory from novice to expert—this pattern might be cause for concern. Understood within a broader and more complex vision of writing growth, this backsliding can be seen as necessary for a student to take a step forward to master new writing forms.

Dyson (cf. 1987, 1989) also described in detail the various paths individual children take in learning to compose, or, in her terms "orchestrat[e] the written language system" (p. 1987, 433). In one study, Dyson (1987) described three emergent writers who each took different routes to becoming proficient writers. They had a few characteristics in common, including their search for order and their desire to make sense as they wrote their initial stories. Simultaneously, they each attended to different aspects of written language at different times and made choices that were consistent with their patterns of interactions with peers and the ways they used writing as a symbolic tool. For instance, one student, Manuel, wrote sentences very slowly. One explanation for his slow pace could be that he paid attention to useless detail or, as Dyson suggested, he was unwilling to copy and use repetitive sentences and thus set a demanding standard for himself. Rather than employing rigid expectations for children at different development stages, Dyson (1987) encouraged us to look "at that whole child working with a complex whole tool [to] see the sense—the music—of each young composer" (p. 440).

QUESTIONS FOR FURTHER DIALOGUE

It is easy to fall into a trap of looking at writing development as being focused solely on the individual or solely on the context. We feel neither to be the case. Instead, a social contextual stance on writing development shifts perspective not away from the individual writer and the individual product but toward seeing that writer and text in multiple contexts. This relation cannot be merely configured as a two-way street between the individuals and their many contexts either. It is far more complicated, interesting, tantalizing, and difficult than that. As writers become cognizant of these various contexts, they also become aware of how these contexts transact with one another, constructing a Bakhtinian dialogue in which the language we own is the language we share, the language we shape is the one that shapes us. Simultaneously, the various identities we bring to writing—racial, ethnic, religious, moral, sexual, and so on—are in dialogue with each other as well as with the text and the composer of that text.

For example, an assigned autobiographical piece written by a Latina adolescent in a rural classroom in northeast Georgia is immersed in a range of contexts: a historical one in terms of that student and that class and a historical context in terms of that genre, a range of cultural identities, a time frame, a voice, an intended real or imagined audience, and a variety of purposes, to name but a few. In addition, there are power relations to consider, many of which are asymmetrical. What is the genre of autobiography and who has a right to determine that? For that matter, what constitutes written text? What language choices need to be considered? What are the conditions for writing and what does it mean to have power over how long in duration and length, with what support, and with what conventions a piece gets written? What are the tensions between the expectations of governing bodies like universities and the world of commerce and the expectations of the expressive individual?

Yet, if we were to conceive of a self-elected memoir being written by an aging European American mother as a keepsake for her children, the resulting text could be very different from that of the Latina teen, far beyond the differing historical data of their lives. What gets said, how it gets said, how much gets said, and with what degree of articulation and engagement would all have potential for variance. This range of difference would occur both despite and because many of the same dimensions would be in play. A sense of writing development must entail a meta-awareness of how these dimensions are implicated in the composing process and an understanding of the impact they have at various times in the process. Although it is probably true that not all these dimensions have equal weight at all times in all cases, it is equally true that learning how to consider and weigh these dimensions is crucial to research in writing development.

Therefore we need to continue to clarify what we mean by writing development. This is a much-used, but seldom-unpacked term. What do we imply when we say we are looking for development in writing? Is it always governed by one set of standards, or do the standards fluctuate? Is it all that we say it is, and could it be other conceptions we have not yet imagined? In at least partial answer to these questions, we offer that furthering our understanding of social contextual issues and how they influence writing development provides opportunities for writers to see themselves as actors in a process that is both personally and socially constructed. This is a continuous, lifelong process.

In essence, we have called for ways to understand writing development in and out of schools in a manner that makes for complexity, something we believe bringing a social lens to writing has done for the field in general. Such a view of writing development offers both the possibilities and frustrations brought on by complexity. The writing classroom is no longer a place where one size fits all, where style and genre are cast in stone, where standard edited English is the only coin of the realm. In such a classroom, continuums and inquiry replace dichotomy and formula. However, through increasing the areas of concern, we impose greater responsibility on both teacher and student. What does it mean in terms of writing development for students to bring their home cultures, peer cultures, popular cultures, and academic cultures, to mention but a few possibilities, to bear on a text in the process of being generated? What does the classroom look like that honors such a range of culture? In what ways is the identity of the individual tied into cultural identities of use (those with which the student already self-identifies), cultural identities of aspiration (those with which the student seeks inclusion), and cultural identities of resistance (those with which the student is reluctant to assume)?

Teachers and learners of writing simultaneously need to grasp the importance of such a stance, because it holds both promise and portent for writing classrooms. The more we understand the ways multiple social dimensions transact with our composing process, the greater facility we will have for using our writing in purposeful and meaningful ways. Alternatively, complex understandings of writing development tend to complicate instruction, curriculum, and assessment, all of which increase the burden on already heavily burdened classroom participants. Therefore, we need to see and learn more about writing development in ways that enable students to take greater control of that development, and not merely unearth complexity for complexity's sake. The challenge for teachers, researchers, and those who consider themselves both is to devise and investigate ways that we can retain this complexity without overwhelming those who must contend with it.

As we consider the many contexts for producing writing, we need to investigate how those contexts can be best explored in school and how out-of-school contexts can supplement and support the work of the school. Accordingly, we wonder what can be learned by imagining and investigating more deeply what it means to write both in and out of the language arts class and in and out of school. What does the transaction of these various contexts allow us to understand about the nature of writing development? Our hope is to see school as a place where writing develops in tandem with other writing experiences beyond the reach of the classroom bell.

Finally, we need to view writing development as being in process. This applies to our theoretical understandings as well as our knowledge of practice (Cochran-Smith & Lytle, in press). From the vantage of theory, what we now know about writing development today will not be what we will know tomorrow. As the nature of writing evolves, particularly as new technology affects our ability to communicate, so will our understanding of what constitutes writing development. From the vantage of implementation, writers need to see themselves as engaging in an ever-widening range of literate practices. As writing and the writer develop, an awareness of context and its relation to oneself also develops. Thus, writers are always in the process of development.

As at least one writing professor in our past has noted, there are no perfect writers. That is the bad news. The good news is that we have our lifetimes to try to get as perfect as we can be, to be in constant approach and proximity to perfection. Imagining the social contextual dimensions of writing as both part of and necessary to understanding writing development enables more of us to have collective agency and support as we seek our individual paths toward our respective falling short of perfection.

ACKNOWLEDGMENTS

We acknowledge the support and suggestions Steve Graham, editor of this special issue, made during various drafts of this article. In addition, we thank Sarah Freedman, Deborah Hicks, Marvin Lazerson, and Susan Lytle for taking much time and effort to provide us with substantive and grounded feedback as the article evolved. Finally, we owe Ruth Ebert our appreciation for her help in readying the final manuscript.

REFERENCES

Atwell, N. (1987). *In the middle: Writing, reading, and learning with adolescents.* Portsmouth, NH: Heinemann.

Bakhtin, M. (1981). *The dialogic imagination* (C. Emerson & M. Holquist, Trans.). Austin: University of Texas Press.

Bakhtin, M. (1986). *Speech genres and other late essays* (V. McGee, Trans.). Austin: University of Texas Press.

Barton, D. (1991). The social nature of writing. In D. Barton & R. Ivanic (Eds.), *Writing in the community* (pp. 1–13). Newbury Park, CA: Sage.

Bizzell, P. (1989). Cultural criticism: A social approach to studying writing. *Rhetoric Review, 7,* 224–230.

Britton, J., Burgess, T., Martin, N., McLeod, A., & Rosen, H. (1975). *The development of writing abilities.* London: Macmillan.

Brodkey, L. (1987). Modernism and the scene(s) of writing. *College English, 49,* 396–418.

Bussis, A. M., Chittenden, E. A., Amarel, M., & Klausner, E. (1985). *Inquiry into meaning: An investigation of learning to read.* Hillsdale, NJ: Lawrence Erlbaum Associates, Inc.

Calkins, L. M. (1986). *The art of teaching writing.* Portsmouth, NH: Heinemann.

Calkins, L. M. (with Harwayne, S.). (1991). *Living between the lines.* Portsmouth, NH: Heinemann.

Carini, P. (1987). *The school lives of seven children.* Grand Forks: North Dakota Monograph Series.

Cazden, C. (1996). Selective traditions: Readings of Vygotsky in writing pedagogy. In D. Hicks (Ed.), *Discourse, learning and schooling* (pp. 165–185). Cambridge, England: Cambridge University Press.

Clark, R., & Ivanic, R. (1997). *The politics of writing.* London: Routledge & Kegan Paul.

Cochran-Smith, M., & Lytle, S. L. (in press). Relationships of knowledge and practice: Teacher learning in communities. In A. Iran-Nejad & C. D. Pearson (Eds.), *Review of research in education.* Washington DC: American Educational Research Association.

Cohen, E. G. (1986). *Designing groupwork: Strategies for the heterogeneous classroom.* New York: Teachers College Press.

Cooper, C., & Odell, L. (1978). *Research on composing: Points of departure.* Urbana, IL: National Council of Teachers of English.

Cooper, M., & Holzman, M. (1989). *Writing as social action.* Portsmouth, NH: Heinemann.

Daiute, C., & Dalton, B. (1988). "Let's brighten it up a bit": Collaboration and cognition in writing. In B. Raforth & D. Rubin (Eds.), *The social construction of written communication* (pp. 249–269). Norwood, NJ: Ablex.

Daiute, C., & Dalton, B. (1992). *Collaboration between children learning to write: Can novices be masters?* (Tech. Rep. No. 60). Berkeley, CA: Center for the Study of Writing.

D'Angelo, F. (1978). An ontological basis for a modern theory of the composing process. *Quarterly Journal of Speech, 64,* 79–85.

Delpit, L. (1995). *Other people's children: Cultural conflict in the classroom.* New York: The New Press.

DiPardo, A., & Freedman, S. W. (1988). Peer response groups in the writing classroom: Theoretical foundations and new directions. *Review of Educational Research, 58,* 119–149.

DuBois, W. E. B. (1961). *The souls of black folk.* New York: Fawcett World Library. (Original work published 1903)

Dyson, A. H. (1987). Individual differences in beginning composing: An orchestral view of learning to compose. *Written Communication, 4,* 411–442.

Dyson, A. H. (1989). *Multiple worlds of child writers: Friends learning to write.* New York: Teachers College Press.

Dyson, A. H. (1990). *The word and the world: Reconceptualizing written language development or do rainbows mean a lot to little girls?* (Tech. Rep. No. 42). Berkeley, CA: Center for the Study of Writing.

Dyson, A. H. (1993). *Social worlds of children learning to write in an urban primary school.* New York: Teachers College Press.

Dyson, A. H. (1995). Writing children: Reinventing the development of childhood literacy. *Written Communication, 12,* 4–46.

Dyson, A. H. (1997). *Writing superheroes: Contemporary childhood, popular culture, and classroom literacy.* New York: Teachers College Press.

Dyson, A. H. (1999). Coach Bombay's kids learn to write: Children's appropriation of media material for school literacy. *Research in the Teaching of English, 33,* 367–402.

Dyson, A. H., & Freedman, S. W. (1991). Writing. In J. Flood, J. Jensen, D. Lapp, & J. Squire (Eds.), *Handbook of research on teaching the English language arts* (pp. 754–775). New York: Macmillan.

Emig, J. (1971). *The composing processes of twelfth graders.* Urbana, IL: National Council of Teachers of English.

Emig, J. (1977). Writing as a mode of learning. *College Composition and Communication, 28,* 122–128.

Fairclough, N. (1989). *Language and power.* London: Longman.

Fecho, B. (1998). Crossing boundaries of race in a critical literacy classroom. In D. Alvermann, K. Hinchman, D. Moore, S. Phelps, & D. Waff (Eds.), *Reconceptualizing the literacies in adolescent lives* (pp. 75–101). Mahwah, NJ: Lawrence Erlbaum Associates, Inc.

Fecho, B. (2000). Critical inquiries into language in an urban classroom. *Research on the Teaching of English, 34*(3), 368–395.

Fiering, S. (1981). Commodore School: Unofficial writing. In D. H. Hymes (Ed.), *Ethnographic monitoring of children's acquisition of reading/language arts skills in and out of the classroom* (Final Report to the National Institute of Education, pp. 51–54). Washington DC: National Institute of Education.

Flower, L. (1989). Cognition, context and theory building. *College Composition and Communication, 40,* 282–311.

Flower, L., & Hayes, J. (1981). A cognitive process theory of writing. *College Composition and Communication, 32,* 365–387.

Foster, M. (1992). Sociolinguistics and the African-American community: Implications for literacy. *Theory into Practice, 31,* 303–311.

Freedman, S. W. (1987). *Response to student writing.* Urbana, IL: National Council of Teachers of English.

Freedman, S. W. (1994a). *Exchanging writing, exchanging culture: Lessons in school reform from the United States and Great Britain.* Cambridge, MA: Harvard University Press.

Freedman, S. W. (1994b). *Moving writing into the 21st century* (Occasional Paper No. 36). Berkeley, CA: National Center for the Study of Writing, University of California, Berkeley, and Carnegie Mellon University.

Freedman, S. W., Dyson, A. H., Flower, L., & Chafe, W. (1987). *Research in writing: Past, present, and future* (Tech. Rep. No. 1–A). Berkeley, CA: National Center for the Study of Writing.

Freedman, S. W., Flower, F., Hull, G., & Hayes, J. R. (1995). *Ten years of research: Achievements of the National Center for the Study of Writing and Literacy* (Tech. Rep. No. 1–C). Berkeley, CA: National Center for the Study of Writing.

Freire, P. (1970). *Pedagogy of the oppressed.* New York: Continuum.

Freire, P. (1985). *The politics of education: Culture, power and liberation.* South Hadley, MA: Bergin & Garvey.

Gee, J. P. (1989). What is literacy? *Journal of Education, 171,* 18–25.

Gee, J. P. (1996). *Social linguistics and literacies: Ideology in discourses* (2nd ed.). London: Falmer.

Gee, J. P., Hull, G., & Lankshear, C. (1996). *The new work order: Behind the language of the new capitalism.* Boulder, CO: Westview.

Gilmore, P. (1983). Spelling "Mississippi": Recontextualizing a literacy event. *Anthropology and Education Quarterly, 14*(4), 235–256.

Giroux, H. (1983). Theories of reproduction and resistance in the new sociology of education: A critical analysis. *Harvard Educational Review, 53,* 527–593.

Goldblatt, E. C. (1995). *'Round my way: Authority and double-consciousness in three urban high school writers.* Pittsburgh: University of Pittsburgh Press.

Graves, D. (1983). *Writing: Teachers and children at work.* Exeter, NH: Heinemann.

Gumperz, J. J. (1981). Conversational inference and classroom learning. In J. Green & C. Wallat (Eds.), *Ethnography and language in educational settings* (pp. 3–23). Norwood: NJ: Ablex.

Hairston, M. (1992). Diversity, ideology, and teaching writing. *College Composition and Communication, 43,* 179–195.

Harste, J. C., Woodward, V. A., & Burke, C. L. (1984). *Language stories and literacy lessons.* Portsmouth, NH: Heinemann.

Heath, S. B. (1983). *Ways with words: Language, life, and work in communities and classrooms.* Cambridge, England: Cambridge University Press.

Heath, S. B., & McLaughlin, M. W. (1993). *Identity and inner-city youth: Beyond ethnicity and gender.* New York: Teachers College Press.

Hicks, D. (1996). Contextual inquiries: A discourse-oriented study of classroom learning. In D. Hicks (Ed.), *Discourse, learning and schooling* (pp.165–185). Cambridge, England: Cambridge University Press.

Hull, G., Jury, M., Ziv, O., & Katz, M. (1996). *Changing work, changing literacy: A study of skill requirements and development in a traditional and a reorganized workplace* (Final Report to the National Center for Research in Vocational Education and the Center for the Study of Writing and Literacy). Berkeley, CA: National Center for Research in Vocational Education.

Hull, G., & Rose, M. (1989). Rethinking remediation: Toward a socio-cognitive understanding of problematic reading and writing. *Written Communication, 6,* 139–154.

Hull, G., & Rose, M. (1990). "This wooden shack place": The logic of an unconventional reading. *College Composition and Communication, 41,* 287–298.

Hull, G., & Schultz, K. (1998). *School's out!: Literacy at work and in the community.* Manuscript in preparation.

Hymes, D. H. (1972). Models of interaction of language and social life. In J. J. Gumperz & D. H. Hymes (Eds.), *Directions in sociolinguistics: The ethnography of communication* (pp. 35–71). New York: Holt, Reinhart & Winston.

Ivanic, R. (1998). *Writing and identity: The discoursal construction of identity in academic writing.* Philadelphia: Benjamins.

Johnson, D. W., & Johnson, R. T. (1987). *Learning together and alone.* Englewood Cliffs, NJ: Prentice Hall.

Kalman, J. (1996). Joint composition: The collaborative letter writing of a scribe and his client in Mexico. *Written Communication, 13,* 190–220.

King, M., & Rentel, V. (1979). Toward a theory of early writing development. *Research in the Teaching of English, 13,* 243–253.

Ladson-Billings, G. (1994). *The Dreamkeepers: Successful teachers of African American children.* San Francisco: Jossey-Bass.

Lensmire, T. J. (1993). Following the child, socioanalysis, and threats to the community: Teacher response to children's texts. *Curriculum Inquiry, 23,* 265–299.

Lensmire, T. J. (1994a). *When children write: Critical re-visions of the writing workshop.* New York: Teachers College Press.

Lensmire, T. J. (1994b). Writing workshop as carnival: Reflections on an alternative learning environment. *Harvard Educational Review, 64,* 371–391.

Lunsford, A. (1979). Cognitive development and the basic writer. *College English, 41,* 449–459.

Lunsford, A., & Ede, L. (1990). *Singular texts/plural authors: Perspectives on collaborative writing.* Carbondale, IL: Southern Illinois University Press.

Lytle, S. L. (1991). Living literacy: Rethinking development in adulthood. *Linguistics and Education, 3,* 109–138.

Lytle, S. L., & Schultz, K. (1990). Assessing literacy learning with adults: An ideological approach. In R. Beach & S. Hynds (Eds.), *Developing dis-*

course processes in adolescence and adulthood (pp. 359–385). Norwood, NJ: Ablex.

Moffett, J. (1968). *Teaching the universe of discourse.* Boston: Houghton Mifflin.

Nystrand, M., Greene, S., & Wiemelt, J. (1993). Where did composition studies come from?: An intellectual history. *Written Communication, 10,* 267–333.

Robinson, T., & Ward, J. V. (1991). "A belief in self far greater than anyone's disbelief": Cultivating resistance among African American female adolescents. In C. Gilligan, A. G. Rogers, & D. L. Tolman (Eds.), *Women, girls, and psychotherapy: Reframing resistance* (pp. 87–103). Binghamton, NY: Harrington Park Press.

Rose, M. (1985). The language of exclusion: Writing instruction at the university. *College English, 47,* 341–359.

Rose, M. (1988). Narrowing the mind and the page: Remedial writers and cognitive reductionism. *College Composition and Communication, 39,* 267–298.

Schultz, K. (1994) "I want to be good; I just don't get it": A fourth-grader's entrance into a literacy community. *Written Communication, 11,* 381–413.

Schultz, K. (1997). "Do you want to be in my story?": Collaborative writing in an urban elementary school classroom. *Journal of Literacy Research, 29,* 253–287.

Schuster, C. (1997). Mikhail Bakhtin as rhetorical theorist. In V. Villanueva, Jr. (Ed.), *Cross talk in composition theory* (pp. 457–473). Urbana, IL: National Council of Teachers of English.

Shaughnessy, M. (1976). Diving in: An introduction to basic writing. *College Composition and Communication, 27,* 234–239.

Shaughnessy, M. (1977). *Errors and expectations.* New York: Oxford University Press.

Slavin, R. (1991). Synthesis of research on cooperative learning. *Educational Leadership, 48*(5), 71–82.

Street, B. (1984). *Literacy in theory and practice.* Cambridge, England: Cambridge University Press.

Street, B. (1995). *Social literacies: Critical approaches to literacy development, ethnography and education.* London: Longman.

Tate, G. (1976). *Teaching composition: 10 bibliographical essays.* Fort Worth: Texas Christian University Press.

Villanueva, V., Jr. (1997). Considerations for American Freristas. In V. Villanueva, Jr. (Ed.), *Cross talk in composition theory* (pp. 621–637). Urbana, IL: National Council of Teachers of English.

Vygotsky, L. (1962). *Thought and language* (E. Hanfmann & G. Vakar, Trans.). Cambridge, MA: MIT Press. (Original work published 1934)

Vygotsky, L. (1978). *Mind and society.* Cambridge, MA: Harvard University Press.

EDUCATIONAL PSYCHOLOGIST, *35*(1), 63
Copyright © 2000, Lawrence Erlbaum Associates, Inc.

List of Reviewers for Volume 35, Number 1

The following list of individuals served as reviewers for this special issue on "Writing Development: The Role of Cognitive, Motivational, and Social/Contextual Factors." The editor and guest editors thank these reviewers for their conscientious service to the journal.

Patricia Alexander
University of Maryland

Stephen Benton
Kansas State University

Robert Calfee
University of California–Riverside

Sarah Freedman
University of California–Berkeley

John Guthrie
University of Maryland

Ronald Kellogg
University of Missouri–Rolla

Charles MacArthur
University of Delaware

Wayne Slater
University of Maryland

Lee Swanson
University of California–Riverside

Bernice Wong
Simon Fraser University

EDUCATIONAL PSYCHOLOGIST, *35*(1), 65

New Editors for *Educational Psychologist*

The Division of Educational Psychology (Division 15) of the American Psychological Association is pleased to announce the new coeditors, Philip H. Winne and Lyn Corno, for the journal *Educational Psychologist*. The new editors will be responsible for the journal beginning with Volume 36, Number 1, to appear in 2001. Manuscripts should be sent to

Philip H. Winne
Coeditor, *Educational Psychologist*
Faculty of Education
Simon Fraser University
Burnaby, British Columbia
Canada V5A 1S6

FOUNDATIONS OF ETHICAL PRACTICE, RESEARCH, AND TEACHING IN PSYCHOLOGY

Karen Strohm Kitchener
University of Denver

The ethical dilemma confronting psychologists in their various roles are becoming more numerous and more complex. Practitioners wondering whether to inform a client's partner of his HIV positive status, researchers trying to study child abuse while maintaining confidentiality, teachers or supervisors balancing their duty to students and their duty to the society in which the students will be credentialled -- all find that formal codes of ethics and existing books do not and cannot address all their concerns and conflicts.

In this book, Karen Kitchener lays a conceptual foundation for thinking well about ethical problems. She introduces a model of decision making based on five underlying principles and illustrates the ways in which it can help psychologists faced with tough choices make ethically defensible decisions. Beyond principled decision making in accordance with codes and her model, she considers the importance of ethical character, and outlines the development of five key virtues that support moral behavior.

Among the thorniest issues she treats in depth are informed consent, confidentiality, both sexual and nonsexual multiple role relationships, competence, and social justice. Throughout, she begins with principles and then shows how they are applied in clinical, educational, and scientific contexts. And throughout, she illuminates her discussion with vivid case examples that reflect her own rich experience and understanding.

Foundations of Ethical Practice, Research, and Teaching in Psychology gives psychologists, students, and trainees the tools they need to analyze their own ethical quandaries and take right action.

Contents: Ethics--What It Is and What Is Not. Thinking Well About Doing Good. Foundational Principles for Thinking Well. Beyond Ethical Decision Making. Respecting Others With Informed Consent. **P.A. Daniel, K.S. Kitchener,** Confidentiality: Doing Good, Avoiding Harm, and Maintaining Trust. Multiple Role Relationships and Conflicts of Interest: Risking Harm. Sexualized Professional Relationships: Causing Harm. Competence: Doing Good and Avoiding Harm. Justice and Social Responsibility: Being Fair and Beyond. **Appendices:** American Psychological Association Ethical Principles of Psychologists and Code of Conduct. Rules and Procedures. Ethics Cases.
0-8058-2309-3 [cloth] / 2000 / 328pp. / $34.95

Lawrence Erlbaum Associates, Inc.
10 Industrial Avenue, Mahwah, NJ 07430
201/236–9500   FAX 201/760–3735

Prices subject to
change without notice.

Call toll-free to order: 1-800-9-BOOKS-9...9am to 5pm EST only.
e-mail to: orders@erlbaum.com
visit LEA's web site at http://www.erlbaum.com

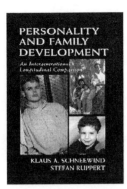

KNOWLEDGE SPACES
Theories, Empirical Research, and Applications
Edited by
Dietrich Albert
Karl-Franzens University, Austria
Josef Lukas
Martin-Luther University, Germany

Based on the formal concept of "knowledge structures" originally proposed by Jean-Claude Falmagne and Jean-Paul Doignon, this book contains descriptions of methodological developments and experimental investigations as well as applications for various knowledge domains. The volume addresses three main topics:

- theoretical issues and extensions of Doignon & Falmagne's theory of knowledge structures;
- empirical validations of specific problem types and knowledge domains, such as sentence comprehension, problem solving in chess, inductive reasoning, elementary mathematical reasoning, and others; and
- application of knowledge structures in various contexts, including knowledge assessment, intelligent tutoring systems, and motor learning.

Unlike most other approaches in the literature in cognitive psychology, this book provides both a rigorous mathematical formulation of knowledge-related psychological concepts and its empirical validation by experimental data.

Contents: J-C. Falmagne, Foreword. **Part I:** *Introduction.* **J. Lukas, D. Albert,** Knowledge Structures: Introduction. **Part II:** *Theoretical Developments and Empirical Investigations.* **D. Albert, T. Held,** Component Based Knowledge Spaces in Problem Solving and Inductive Reasoning. **M. Schrepp, T. Held, D. Albert,** Component Based Construction of Surmise Relations for Chess Problems. **T. Held,** An Integrated Approach for Constructing, Coding, and Structuring a Body of Word-Problems. **K. Korossy,** Modeling Knowledge as Competence and Performance. **M. Schrepp,** An Empirical Test of a Process Model for Letter Series Completion Problems. **Part III:** *Applications.* **K. Korossy,** Organizing and Controlling Learning Processes Within Competence-Performance Structures. **D. Albert, M. Schrepp,** Structure and Design of an Intelligent Tutorial System Based on Skill Assignments. **S. Narciss,** Application of Doignon and Falmagne's Theory of Knowledge Spaces to the Assessment of Motor Learning Processes.
0-8058-2799-4 [cloth] / 1999 / 256pp. / $49.95
Special Prepaid Offer! $24.50
No further discounts apply.

Lawrence Erlbaum Associates, Inc.
10 Industrial Avenue, Mahwah, NJ 07430
201/236–9500   FAX 201/760–3735

Prices subject to
change without notice.

Call toll-free to order: 1-800-9-BOOKS-9...9am to 5pm EST only.
e-mail to: orders@erlbaum.com
visit LEA's web site at http://www.erlbaum.com

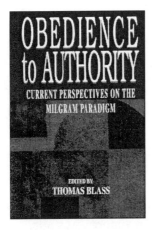

OBEDIENCE TO AUTHORITY
Current Perspectives on the Milgram Paradigm

Edited by

Thomas Blass
University of Maryland, Baltimore County

Stanley Milgram's experiments on obedience to authority are among the most important psychological studies of this century. Perhaps because of the enduring significance of the findings -- the surprising ease with which ordinary persons can be commanded to act destructively against an innocent individual by a legitimate authority -- it continues to claim the attention of psychologists and other social scientists, as well as the general public. The study continues to inspire valuable research and analysis. The goal of this book is to present current work inspired by the obedience paradigm.

Obedience to Authority: Current Perspectives on the Milgram Paradigm demonstrates the vibrancy of the obedience paradigm by presenting some of its most important and stimulating contemporary uses and applications. Paralleling Milgram's own eclecticism in the content and style of his research and writing, the contributions comprise a potpourri of styles of research and presentation, ranging from personal narratives, through conceptual analyses, to randomized experiments.

Contents: Preface. **A. Milgram,** My Personal View of Stanley Milgram. **H. Takooshian,** How Stanley Milgram Taught About Obedience and Social Influence. **J. Waters,** Professor Stanley Milgram--Supervisor, Mentor, Friend. **T. Blass,** The Milgram Paradigm After 35 Years: Some Things We Now Know About Obedience to Authority. **B.E. Collins, L. Ma,** Impression Management and Identity Construction in the Milgram Social System. **F. Rochat, A. Modigliani,** Captain Paul Grueninger: The Chief of Police Who Saved Jewish Refugees by Refusing to Do His Duty. **E. Tarnow,** Self-Destructive Obedience in the Airplane Cockpit and the Concept of Obedience Optimization. **A.L. Saltzman,** The Role of the Obedience Experiments in Holocaust Studies: The Case for Renewed Visibility. **C. Marsh,** A Science Museum Exhibit on Milgram's Obedience Research: History, Description, and Visitors' Reactions. **F. Rochat, O. Maggioni, A. Modigliani,** The Dynamics of Obeying and Opposing Authority: A Mathematical Model. **P.G. Zimbardo, C. Maslach, C. Haney,** Reflections on the Stanford Prison Experiment: Genesis, Transformations, Consequences.
0-8058-2737-4 [cloth] / 2000 / 264pp. / $59.95

Special Prepaid Offer! $34.50
No further discounts apply.

Lawrence Erlbaum Associates, Inc.
10 Industrial Avenue, Mahwah, NJ 07430
201/236–9500   FAX 201/760–3735

Prices subject to change without notice.

Call toll-free to order: 1-800-9-BOOKS-9...9am to 5pm EST only.
e-mail to: orders@erlbaum.com
visit LEA's web site at http://www.erlbaum.com

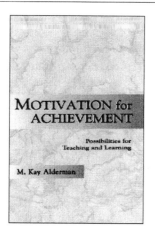